Tales from a Small
RUGBY CLUB

Chris "gus" Chesney

Printed in the United States of America.

Library of Congress Control Number: 2019907256

ISBN	Paperback	978-1-64361-733-6
	Hardback	978-1-64361-734-3
	eBook	978-1-64361-735-0

Westwood Books Publishing LLC
10389 Almayo Ave, Suite 103
Los Angeles, CA 90064

www.westwoodbookspublishing.com

CONTENTS

INTRODUCTION

I hate to admit it but I'm not a lover of books about rugby. Whilst I'll admit I don't actually go into bookshops looking for such books, those that I have seen or that come my way by other means just don't grab my interest. With the exception of those wonderful books by Michael Green about "Coarse Rugby" that were popular in the 1960s, most publications on rugby seem to fall into three groups. Firstly, there are those of a quasi-technical nature, including mind-numbing details of tours made by international teams and the diagram-filled coaching manuals for nerds. Next, there are the personal "autobiographies" written for outstanding recently-retired players of immense renown. Lastly, there are the collections of what are claimed to be amusing and pithy asides by the great and good. These latter books seem to be universally left in home toilets for reading by those forced to stay there for a lengthy period because of extreme digestional difficulties. Come to think of it, the bog is probably far and away the best place to leave such collections of what are mostly distinctly lacking in any real humour or wit; at least they'd provide a fall-back Plan B in the case of emergencies, although the paper would probably cut your arse to ribbons.

The point of this personal rant is that none of these books reflect the wonderful times and experiences that I enjoyed when a player in the late 1950s through to the early 1970s. Nor, for those of you that will immediately claim that the game has altered dramatically since then, during my subsequent involvements as a referee, a coach and as a treasurer of a club. Yes, the game of rugby has indeed changed, as has society in general, but the manner in which it is played in the smaller rugby clubs, plus the attitudes of the players involved, both on and off the field, seem very little different to me. The truly nonsensical and, viewed dispassionately with late-arriving adulthood from a few decades later, the sometimes pretty anti-social exploits in which I was involved don't seem that far apart from those performed with great gusto by my two sons this century.

To me, the most important thing to keep in mind is that rugby is a game; no more, no less. And like all games its value is in providing enjoyment and entertainment to all those who participate. But for me, the most heart-warming aspect of rugby has been the friendships that I've built up over the years; friendships so strong that I can still go visit a clubhouse or a pub that I've not been inside for not just years but decades and can meet there people with whom I can immediately re-kindle a relationship as if we'd last met just yesterday.

This book, then, is my attempt to soften and humanise the manner in which rugby is portrayed by other, probably more worthy tomes; to share the glee and the mischief which was and continues to be enjoyed by all those involved. And if any of my friends, acquaintances, fellow club members and former opponents suspect that, in the stories that follow, they can discern references to themselves by which they have been unfairly characterised, or I have deliberately misrepresented, maligned or even insulted them – excellent.

IN THE BEGINNING

Why does anyone become not just attracted to any particular sport but totally absorbed if not besotted by it? Regarded dispassionately, no sport is "better" than any other, they are all equally good. Certainly, some sports command a wider audience than others, such as Association Football, or soccer, as compared with Rugby Football. Even if you combined the total number of followers of Rugby Union and Rugby League, and then added in the adherents to Australian Rules and Gaelic Football, the resulting grand total would still be swamped by the comparative numbers of soccer supporters. Indeed, that would still be the case if all the US citizens that avidly follow American Football were added to the number of fans of the mish-mash of the other games that not only permit but encourage and concentrate on handling the ball. And that's despite continuing to include the word "football" in their various titles.

Nevertheless, my heart had been lost to rugby from a very young age, to the virtual exclusion of all other winter ball games. Why? I suppose that the primary reason was not only that my father played rugby but that, from a very early age, he would take me with him on every Saturday afternoon, whether he was playing at home or away. At the time this practice started, I must have been about eight or nine and I suspect I accompanied him because my mother had two younger sons to look after, nearly six and eight years younger than me, and she probably felt that for my father to swan off from midday Saturday until late that evening, leaving her with three young boys to cope with was pushing his luck far too far. Whatever the true reason, I spent just about every winter's Saturday afternoon with my father for at least four or five years.

Even still, I did not experience an Ephesus moment impelling me to play rugby from watching my father play. Frankly, I didn't have a clue what he and the up to other 29 players and the referee were doing out on the pitch. Soccer is a wonderfully simple game that, as we all know and have probably personally experienced, can be played by children from a very early age, needing only an open space, a football, at least two children and a couple of coats to act as goalposts to play. Rugby, by comparison with the flowing simplicity of football, is a very staccato affair, constrained by numerous and, to a child, wholly illogical laws and equally mysterious interpretations. Furthermore, whereas soccer can easily be played without a referee, rugby would be extremely difficult to play without such an arbitrator. In consequence, watching Kipling's very "muddied oafs at the goals" was wholly incomprehensible to me and, it often seemed, also to many of the participants. Instead, I and the children of other members of both teams would devise a rugby-like game of our own making. Even so, it bore a very close resemblance to that being played by our fathers, consisting of very little passing of the ball but a lot of uncomplicated, completely result-less wrestling for it, mostly in various depths of mud.

Not having any definitive objective to our game made no difference to our enjoyment; being left alone to roll in the mud without any immediate recrimination was extremely exhilarating. Not only that but, when I finally returned home on each Saturday evening, my mother seemed to accept my muddy and dishevelled state as being worth the price of my extended absence and, even when I returned in some disarray, would only mildly remonstrate with me.

No, my affection for rugby came from a very early age from being welcomed into what for me was a magical circle, a gathering of grown-ups who treated me, almost without exception, with much affection and tolerance. Playing away was an even more enjoyable experience. My father was an extremely enthusiastic second-row forward but even the most charitable onlooker would not have described him as being particularly skilled. As a result, he was regularly picked for his club's "Extra A", or third team. Not that he was in any way upset by this; it meant he'd be playing with his friends from school who were also, often, his friends from the Territorial Army and therefore also from his war years before he was posted to Africa. Even so, I now have a fairly strong suspicion that a major, contributing factor to his regular and completely dependable selection for the Extra A XV was the fact that he was not only exceptional in those post World War 2 years in owning a private car but also that it was a large, just post-war, American Ford V8 Pilot station wagon. My father had purchased this from a US serviceman who brought it with him from his home in the States and who was now returning there but saw no need to also repatriate his vehicle. For us, as a family, this was an ideal vehicle. It meant that, every Sunday, we could venture forth with our extended family of uncles, aunts and cousins, up to fifteen of us, all crammed onto the three, wide bench-seats inside this car. Similarly, although it was only used to transfer an entire rugby team on very infrequent occasions, it did mean that the team captain could virtually guarantee turning up at an away match with at least the strong nucleus of a XV if my father had been selected to play.

Normally, these away fixtures could be accommodated if at least two players possessed cars. My father's would take about nine or ten players, plus their kit, and his entourage would be completed by myself and two or three other children. The other car, from memory, was usually an enormous Humber Super Snipe which, to we children, had a marvellous attraction as being in our eyes the nearest thing we'd actually seen that resembled the vehicles used for transporting illicit booze in the films we saw at the cinema about US gang wars. This huge vehicle was owned by Graham who, himself, had an aura of romantic mystery about him, at least to we children. Allegedly, as was told to me in later years, he had signed up to join the Royal Navy in the last year or so of World War 2, even though he was only 15 at the time. This had resulted in him becoming a stoker on a ship that went to Egypt, where Graham distinguished himself by winning an inter-services Speedway Cup, of all things. How true some of Graham's other reminiscences were I neither knew then or even now, but he certainly owned a large, somewhat battered and tarnished silver cup whose inscription confirmed it had been awarded for such an achievement.

If it seems more than a little fanciful for just two vehicles to transport an entire rugby team plus three or four children to an away fixture which, in even those days would be up to sixty miles away, that's because you're assuming that my father's team always had fifteen players. Truth is, that would be regarded as a luxury. More typically, the lower teams of any small rugby club could often only muster twelve or thirteen players, sometimes even less. Indeed, I can distinctly remember one occasion when we travelled, to Colchester I think it was, with only eight players, and the capabilities of some of those were questionable. Why, I can hear you ask, drive over forty miles to play a game with only just over half a team? Because no-one ever thought of cancelling it, that's why. All those travelling (well, most of them) had been looking forward to this game and the subsequent revelries in the opposing team's clubhouse all week, and the host team were bound to have some spares they'd lend us, wouldn't they?

And that would indeed generally be the case. In the lower teams, it was usually the older players who were the stalwarts, the married men with their children, for whom from about midday on Saturdays, whether playing rugby in the winter or cricket in the summer, these events were considered so precious and essential to their well-being that they were to be carried out no matter the obstacles. Younger members, especially those who had only just left school, were much less inclined to be parted from the current love of their life for even a few minutes of their Saturday evenings. In consequence, these less committed individuals, especially if their skills and enthusiasm for the battle was not exactly whole-hearted, could normally be relied upon to make up their minds about playing only just before mid-day on the Saturday, when their plans for the evening had proved over-optimistic. They'd then drift up to the clubhouse, shortly before kick-off, to see if there was any chance of a game. And, of course, there always was. Not to play in any key position, mind, but mostly out on the wing where they could pretty well rely upon the ball never reaching either them or their opposite number and thus ensuring neither would be required to engage in any nasty, head-on physical confrontation and violence. All they were likely to need to do was to collect the ball when it went into touch and to subsequently throw it into the ensuing line-out.

Mind you, doing this did require, if you had any knowledge of and experience in wing play, a not inconsiderable amount of both tactical and technical skills. Forget what you see on television, or even demonstrated by the higher teams in club rugby, as the ball was most often kicked into touch for health and safety reasons, especially when nearing the final whistle. By that time, especially amongst the older forwards, who had almost always graduated from the back row through the second row to the front row as age inevitably took its toll, legs were becoming disinclined to move at any speed above a begrudging stroll and breathing had become akin to that required to making the final push to the summit of Everest. It was therefore critical that the ball was not put back into play too quickly, especially as getting an ambulance to the pitches out in the back of beyond where the lower teams of small rugby clubs play could be a considerable challenge. Thus, it was the winger's duty to carefully delay retrieving the ball. This was sometimes fairly easy, especially if it had landed in a nearby canal or in an adjoining field that had been set aside specifically for the cultivation of emperor-size nettles.

All this would be done without any complaint from the opposition. After all, it would usually be them that had kicked the ball into touch, thus demonstrating their own fragile, composite state of being. Nowadays, with the much superior fitness of players, such weakness would be seized upon immediately and a line-out taken as soon as possible. Back in those days of yore however, everyone was only too keen to take advantage of the possibility to defer, if only for a minute or so, the serious likelihood of the collapse of a more elderly player; or even some of the younger ones, come to think of it.

Thus the lower teams of most clubs would often play games of 12 or 13 a side, and sometimes as few as 11. But, given all this occurred long before leagues were introduced into Rugby Union, nobody really cared. And when the game was over and the players trudged wearily but generally happily from the pitch, the mud-spattered forwards individually surrounded in personal cocoons of steam and the backs often completely unadorned by mud, this was the time to which we children really looked forward; tea.

Since the end of World War 2, the facilities provided for playing sport of most kinds has improved out of sight. These days, at least as far as Rugby Union is concerned, even the smallest and most modest clubs have clubhouses of which to be proud and, in the majority of cases, located on the grounds themselves. Back in the late 1940s and early 1950s though, this was seldom the case, at least for minor clubs. Then, a large number of clubs of this nature had entered into a pact with a local pub whereby, in exchange for providing access to a room in which the players could change, both before and after their games, the pub would reap the benefit of the sudden influx, in the late afternoon or early evening, of considerably more patrons than ordinarily would be the case, and all of whom were desperately in need of substantial volumes of beer.

There were a few drawbacks to this arrangement, even so. Quite often, the pub involved would not be located on the ground but a good few minutes' walk away. Not only that, but it was not uncommon for the pitches to be located in a public park where, although the local authority might have condescended to allowing rugby to be played there, naturally for an annual rent payable in advance, it would not supply the necessary goal posts or cross-bars. These had to be stored at the back of the pub's car park and carried to and from the ground. There, they had to be erected (and getting the cross-bar on was always a bugger) and, after the game, taken down. And having to carry them back to the pub when pretty exhausted and liberally daubed in mud, especially on a dark December evening with the wind howling around you and the rain lashing down, was not something greatly to be wished. That was when we children came to learn a lot of short new words that had such an emphatic tone to them.

But I digress. Another element of the entente cordiale between a rugby club and its pub was the provision of a meal after the match. This, initially, as I remember it, was not something that the pubs were keen on providing. Back then, very few pubs provided anything of substance to eat to their customers; crisps (the old Smiths' packets, with salt separately included within the bag in a little blue twist of paper) or maybe arrowroot biscuits were about the full and exhaustive range of their most imaginative culinary offerings. And as for different flavours of crisps, there was potato and that was it. What more did you expect? This is a pub, mate; people come here to get pissed. And even "people" was a misnomer; the clientele was almost exclusively male. Any woman present, unless clearly attached to a male customer, was instantly rumoured to be "on the game".

But the pubs soon realised that it would be entirely in their own interests to provide a meal to their rugby-playing guests, even if only sandwiches and cups of tea. It was all a matter of economics. The games of rugby would finish, depending on the daylight hours in the month, at between 3.45 pm and 4.45 pm. Given that the minimal washing facilities at the pub (say two cracked hand-basins to accommodate anything up to sixty men, and with hot water not on the menu), the players would be ready and eager to start the evening's entertainment by between 4.30 pm and 5.30 pm. And therein lay the rub; the pub's opening hour was not until 6.00 pm. You see the problem? Thus the pubs, more than a little desirous to open up the evening with a pub full of rugby players suffering from acute and advanced de-hydration, plus a raging thirst, had to ensure they did not drift off elsewhere for the widely perceived necessity of getting some solid food in your stomach before embarking on what it would be hoped would be an evening of incredible and life-enhancing debauchery, however much past experience would conclude that the likelihood of realising such dreams was almost non-existent.

So, for we children, this was the highlight of the afternoon. Whilst our fathers were doing as best they could to cleanse themselves of the detritus of the pitches with freezing cold water before changing back into their street wear, we would be ushered into, typically, the saloon bar (well, rugby players were gentlemen, weren't they?). There, the small round tables it contained would have large plates of sandwiches ready and waiting. When I think of their contents today, their appeal seems distinctly muted: spam, corned beef, fish paste, and strawberry jam, all on margarine, come readily to mind. Yet to our pretty simple, unsophisticated and inexperienced palates, this was about as good as it got. Especially as we had first pick of the sandwiches, before our elders and betters arrived.

But even these wonderful experiences paled if your father was playing away against a team from a club formed for its workforce by one of the more enlightened manufacturing employers. Admittedly, there were not a large number of these but one that remains pristine and without equal in my memories was Briggs Motor Bodies Sports Club. This was a company that was a sub-contractor to the Ford Motor Company, and supplied it with body parts. Whilst I can no longer remember exactly where it was located, it had to be somewhere reasonably close to the Ford plant at Dagenham. Not only did Briggs Sports have their own rugby and soccer pitches on ground adjacent to their manufacturing plant, but they also had changing rooms with a large communal bath and, wait for it, a separate shower area. And all these facilities actually had hot water; can you believe that? But the piece de resistance was that they had their very own, purpose-built clubhouse capable of satisfying the needs of both the rugby and soccer players who had enjoyed their playing facilities that afternoon. Not only that but, wonder of wonders, they had their own kitchens and would therefore provide all the players with hot food after their games!

Admittedly, the meals were pretty simple: sausages, mash and beans, or fried fish and chips, or rissoles and chips, for example. I was never too sure about rissoles; I never knew exactly what they were (and still don't, to this day) but suspect I was more than a little prejudiced when about nine at the whispered advice from one of my father's team-mates that they were "Arseholes, kid; arseholes". I wasn't sure whether to believe him or not but it seemed prudent to give rissoles a wide berth. So all we children had not just a cooked, evening meal, but plenty of it. Once everyone had been served, players and spectators alike, the ladies in the kitchen would bring around the large metal containers in which the food had been cooked in large industrial ovens to see if anyone wanted another helping before whatever was left was thrown away. In my memories these ladies were always wonderfully jolly and hospitable since they always first approached any children sitting at the tables amongst the adults, usually fully encouraged by the adults themselves. To we children, this largesse was something not to be refused nor forgotten as most of us would normally only receive one cooked meal a day, and that was at mid-day. Evening meals, called tea, supper or dinner, usually only consisted of sandwiches, and sometimes just bread and margarine or, better by far, bread and the dripping taken from the Sunday joint. At this point I can actually feel my sons raising their eyebrows in mute exasperation. Excellent; I'm feeling more Dickensian by the minute.

Then, after we'd all eaten and washed it down with tea served from an enormous urn in great, thick white china cups, there was the final coup de grace. Just above head-height, at one end of the clubhouse, away from the bar that would shortly open to initially serve only large jugs of beer to the various captains to take around, firstly, to the opposing teams' players, was a television. That's what I said, a television, really and truly. And it wasn't one of those piddly little nine inch jobs like the family across the road had – it was enormous! At least a fifteen inch job! Once the plates and other debris of the meals had been cleared away, the television was switched on. I'm sure that it was used for other programmes but I can only remember it being used for sports results, and these consisted solely of the results of the day's horse races and, far more importantly, those of the soccer games. As soon as the screen changed to show all the matches scheduled, with the scores appearing as the calm measured tones of John Snagge or his contemporise began to read them out, those present who had not already prepared themselves reached into their pockets or wallets to extract their football pools papers. These would be checked with extreme care amid a hushed silence, with any hooligan making more than a miniscule of noise being immediately shouted down. Sadly, over the years, I never experienced anyone who claimed to have won anything. Of course, there could have been some but they, given the number of both friends and total strangers present who would doubtless have responded to any joyous acclamation with demands that the lucky winner provide beers all round, may well have decided that discretion was the better part of a very short period of affluence.

Thereafter, we children would be left to amuse ourselves for a couple of hours or more whilst our fathers gradually congregated around the bar area. From the very start of such social intercourse it was all quite noisy and boisterous but this was as nothing compared to the singing into which virtually everybody entered a little while later. Why this should obviously provide all these adults such enjoyment was difficult to understand; the singing was raucous rather than harmonious and often seemed to be about parts of the anatomies of both ladies and gentlemen I never heard mention in ordinary conversations.

Eventually, there came a moment when, by common unspoken consent, after much glancing at watches, it was time to go home. Bags of kit were gathered, good-byes said, hands shaken, promises given to "stuff you next year" and we all made our way to the two vehicles in which we'd come. Sometimes, and not that uncommonly, it would then be realised that Graham and his car had gone, it normally being rather shamefacedly explained subsequently by that worthy that he'd been on a promise from one of his numerous and slightly seedy lady friends – hadn't he mentioned it before? No, the bastard hadn't but, whatever the reason, it could leave my father with the irritation of having to accommodate maybe up to another three or four people in his already over-crowded vehicle. Sometimes, despite all the will in the world, this would not prove to be possible and the unfortunate modern castaway would be left, sullen and with readily-apparent homicidal tendencies, to get to the local railway station before beginning the journey home, hopefully that night.

As for me, I didn't care. I was bomb-proof; it was my father's car. Better still, if the day had been eventful for me already, the journey home would be something else. On the way up, slightly less laden, we'd got to our destination without any intervening stops. Achieving that on the way back always proved to be impossible. Firstly, there were the absolutely critical halts required for medical necessities. These, mostly to employ urinary glands, were frequent and generally accepted as being understandable. Even if only one passenger was suddenly to claim in almost frenzied desperation that, unless he could have a piss instantly, there would a tragic accident, once my father had swerved into the nearest lay-by, there was a mass movement out of the car to the nearest hedge. There, legs apart, standing in a long line with clouds of steam billowing in front of them, would stand my fellow passengers, although my father would companionably join them.

This well-appreciated and practised ceremony would occur about every ten or so miles all the way home. Less sympathy, however, would be afforded to another physical ailment. Particularly when my father's car was more crowded than usual, I'd be sitting on one of my father's team-mates' laps, jammed against the other occupants of either the second or third bench seats of the vehicle. Snug it may have been but comfortable, not exactly. Almost inevitably in such circumstances, someone would suddenly scream in agony as cramp set in. Additionally, in throwing himself about to lessen the pain, the sufferer would inevitably kick someone else or, in an involuntary reaction, jerk his elbow sharply backwards, usually into the face of his wholly unprepared neighbour, and these worthies would also let out bellows of pain and flail about.

If anyone outside the vehicle had been able to dispassionately watch the happenings inside, it's difficult to know how they would have interpreted such goings-on. A party from the local lunatic asylum on a night out? A yummy mummy taking home a gang of school kids after a birthday treat? The local Liberal Party on its annual get-together? No, it's just a team of rugby players making their way home in a grossly over-crowded vehicle. Oh, that's all right then.

These and other mishaps and incongruous events meant that, to me, Saturdays spent with my father could never be described as dull. They were always full of fun and unexpected excitement, often from the most bizarre occurrences. Is it any wonder then that I became hooked on rugby and determined to follow my father's footsteps? Furthermore, perhaps I'd then learn what all those songs were about.

THE FRONT ROW UNION

This particular, educational section is for those of you who didn't or haven't played rugby and, most particularly, not in the front row of the forwards. For those that did or have, what I'm about to state is generally pretty self-evident. To my mind, all sport is to be encouraged, for any number of reasons. No sport is any better, in truth, than any other; all of them have tremendous attributes that make them beneficial contributors to a well-adjusted society. However, before proceeding further, I think I should better clarify who, in rugby, are the members of the co-called Front Row Union. Props, both tight-head and loose-head, definitely; hookers? I'm not so sure. In my experience (and in many of those shared with me by other props) there is more than a suspicion that hookers all have mental failings of one sort or another. With some hookers, these are only revealed occasionally; with others, it can be such an ongoing demonstration of retardation that you wonder if the team's communal kit should not contain a straight-jacket for their wacky behaviour that can almost be forecast to occur off the field. And on it, come to that.

During a game, almost every hooker I've come across is a loud-mouthed, obnoxious rabble-raiser; and that's on a better day. The only other position whose players can challenge hookers for gratuitously insulting and objectionable behaviour is that of scrumhalf. Most forwards come to the conclusion by one means or another that scrumhalves are all born with a Napoleon complex. They're typically stunted in size and nearly wholly unappreciative of the fact that rugby is a team game. Straining might and main in a scrum on a filthy wet afternoon is bad enough in itself but being constantly nagged at by a scrumhalf for being lazy, fat bastards does not uplift the soul. And this nagging is being done by your own scrumhalf. Certainly, one of the most sublime and exquisite joys for a pack of forwards is to catch and place a scrumhalf at the bottom of a ruck. Preferably that of the opposition, but not necessarily so. Believe me, I say this not because I have an inbuilt dislike and contempt of scrumhalves; some of my best friends played in that position. Those that are still alive, anyway.

But back to the front row. Forwards have to be contented with the less glamorous and far more prosaic elements of rugby, not like the big girls' blouses that ponce around in the three-quarters, desperate not to get their kit wet or dirty. And those forwards that constantly have to face the greatest physical challenges are the Front Row Union. I know the second row is where the enforcers normally reside, but their heads are comfortably cushioned between the often lumpish hips of those in the front row; they don't have their heads driven into their shoulders by their opposite numbers who are suffering from galloping halitosis and who are eating raw garlic to combat it. Nevertheless, although it's true that there is a strong bond of comradeship amongst members of the Front Row Union, generally for life, you can only gain entrance once you've passed a very rigorous and testing physical and mental examination. Now, we're not mindless, vicious, wholly insensitive animals, despite what has been written and said totally without merit by others. For example, one of New Zealand's sports columnists stated, back in 2003, that, "They're raw-boned, cauliflower-eared monoliths that ran on to the field like white orcs on steroids." Now, how unfair is that? And wholly inaccurate; get your facts right, Mr. Lewis – most of us didn't even know what steroids were, unless they were those things you shoved up your arise if you had piles.

Anyway, a newly arrived, would-be permanent member of a front row would be afforded every courtesy, at least for the first scrums whilst the rest of us sized him up. Most often, he would be a recent school-leaver and they came in two major varieties. Firstly there was the young blood that'd been quite a whiz at school and fancied himself as merely playing in a lower team whilst he impressed both his team-mates and the selectors with his prowess, both in the set-pieces and around the field. This unfortunately mis-conceived self-esteem would have come from playing schoolboy rugby at county, area or even national level but, to be honest, it meant bugger-all to the rest of us. This is real rugby, son. Even so, if he showed he was prepared to work hard at the coal-face and serve his apprenticeship he'd probably get by without too much personal pain, hardship and insult. Sometimes, anyway; it all depended on how pretty he was when he first packed down.

The other school-leaver was the lad who'd ultimately be welcomed into the Front Row Union with open arms; initially deferential and willing to learn as well as showing no inclination to fart around the field like the three-quarters. And if he ever got the ball in his hands, he was expected to either drop it or throw it forward immediately. Better still, if he could learn to chuck the ball sideways without looking, hopefully smack into the face of a three-quarter haring up beside him at speed that would get him bonus points. However, to develop that last skill he'd have to hang out with members of the second row; that was an ability that most of them had been born with.

The other new recruit to the front row would usually be temporary, someone enticed into the game with no prior experience whatsoever. If such individual looked nervous and skinny, he was immediately assured that the best place to watch and learn the intricacies and subtle nuances of the game would be the wing, and out to the barren wastes he'd be posted, far from the madding crowd. But for the new recruit that appeared squat, over-weight and gormless, why, he was ideal front row material. Sadly, despite these knowing, unseen evaluations of the inherent likely capabilities of new recruits of this nature, they were often completely wrong. I know of one such player, skinny and fragile, who was told to play on the wing who ultimately graduated to captaining his club's first XV from the second row. As shy and demure as he appeared at that first off-field evaluation, once he trotted out onto the pitch it was as if an internal switch had been thrown. He became an absolute lunatic, jumping around like a fire-cracker and continually popping up in places where he had no right to be. Worse still, he kept exhorting the forwards to keep up with him. Keep up with him? We couldn't even work out where he'd be shooting off to next, bloody fool.

In any event, if these new recruits proved to have some promise, they gradually learned, mostly by hard and painful experience, most of the tricks of the trade. If not, since their intellects were obviously not up to it, they'd probably be switched to playing at wing-forward, where they could do less harm.

Once, then, you entered a match with a tried and tested front row, your first objective would be to try out that of the opposing team. In the line-outs, this was comparatively simple; you simply looked to see if any large gaps were left between their jumper and his supporting prop forward. Not only that, but to see if the prop was unwise and inexperienced enough to turn his head upwards, unguarded, to see if his jumper had, wonder of wonders, actually caught the ball. Thus, if a large gap had been left between them, it would not be difficult to insert a hand, an arm or even an elbow therein and, in strenuous efforts to dislodge the ball, accidently catch the prop on the nose or, even more satisfying, the jumper in his balls. Although this was not that difficult to achieve, it had the distinct disadvantage of being performed in the comparative open, in clear view of the referee. Of more subsequent potential personal harm, it was also easier for the other members of the opposing team to observe, whereas what happened amongst the Front Row Union in the scrum was much more difficult to discern.

These days, when the scrum goes down, the revisions made to the laws over the last forty years or so are supposed to ensure that the scrum stays steady and that the forwards pack down in such a way that their hips and heads remain in a straight line parallel to the ground. This rarely happens now and very seldom happened before. Whilst an admirable objective (and one that should still be sought), it is not that often achieved even in Rugby Sevens, when only three forwards pack down from either side. If you then add another five players to each side, with all their inevitable individual variances in height, weight, age, health, degree of aggression and ability, it is not just no wonder that scrums collapse, but that they ever stay up long enough for the ball to be put in. Frankly, forwards should be roundly applauded and idolised for the manner in which they enable contested scrums to be completed, not roundly criticised, condemned and excoriated by former players, mostly wimps from the threes.

In my playing days, little was different. But then, we played to the laws such that the ball was actually put in straight, between the front rows and the hookers both struck for the ball, aided by their props. Accordingly, at the first scrum, immediately upon the ball being put in, both the hooker and the prop on the side of the scrum where the ball was put in would strike for the ball. The primary purpose was, ostensibly, to gain possession of the ball for your team but at least a major secondary objective was to severely hack the shins and ankles of your opposite number. This was not mindless brutality (well, not that much) but a cunning tactical ploy. Once you'd managed to hack shit out of your immediate opponent's shins you'd virtually be able to rely on him keeping his shins and ankles out of reach of any further assaults you'd make. Thus, at first assessment, you'd get a pretty good idea of how tough a match you'd have in the scrums. If you looked at the lower legs of your opposite number and he was wearing clean socks and cutaway boots with go-fast stripes that all showed off the elegant turn of his ankle, you knew you were in for an easy afternoon; you'd be playing against a pussy cat. But if your immediate opponent wore at least two pairs of socks, with the outside pair rolled down to protect his ankles, thick shin-pads and old, heavy leather boots with steel toe-caps and extended upper parts that came up to almost cover the ankles from below, you'd be facing a tried and tested front row warrior with legs whose shape would not have disgraced a snooker table, and it was clearly going to be an epic battle.

Without such a gnarled and fearsome opponent, if you'd forced the prop opposite you to chicken out and keep his ankles and shins clear of your onslaughts, it meant that at every subsequent scrum you'd be free to strike for the ball and thus help your hooker trap it in a pincer movement. This all worked best when the scrums were upright, because that enabled the hooker and the prop concerned to stand on just one leg. The defence to this ploy was for the other front row to drop the scrum so low that you had to have both feet on the ground unless you wanted to nose-dive into the turf. It also gave the hooker whose side would be putting the ball into the scrum the advantage that, his head being nearest the ball, the opposing hooker's view of the ball would be completely blocked. One problem with this defence though, was that it would be virtually physically impossible to hook the ball with your face about an inch above the turf when in a crouched position and with your arms wrenched above your body whilst clutching onto your props. Not surprisingly, especially if the scrumhalf was farting about and failed to put the ball in quickly, the law of gravity would prevail and both front rows would collapse head-first into the mud. Very few players could ever do anything else. Only one that I ever came across was the Irish hooker, Ken Kennedy. In a county championship match, when I was desperately trying to hold up my opposite prop whilst the angle of my body from the waist had rendered breathing impossible, Ken would hook the ball back every time. Mind you, I strongly believe he did it with his nose.

When a scrum had collapsed, though, we'd then struggle to our feet and, after sour and venomous glares at the scrumhalf responsible and snarled urgings to "Put the fucking ball in, will you", we'd get down and try again. As iconic as that renowned photograph of a black-faced Fran Cotton is, that was as nothing compared to the two front rows preparing for yet another confrontation on a muddy, cow-pack infested field out in the back of nowhere.

Things have changed materially these days, with referees virtually allowing scrumhalves to roll the ball into the scrum diagonally, so that it's virtually impossible for the opposing hooker to get his foot anywhere near the ball. No wonder a naive England hooker has just been reported as stating that, until recently, when referees appeared to decide to actually but only temporarily apply this law, if only for half of a season before they returned to their previous lazy, ignorant interpretation, he had never had to hook a ball before. Why the fuck did he think that the position is called "Hooker"?

In my day, the referees were literate and could both read and understand the laws of Rugby Union. Back then, referees understood that, for those that played in the front row, the contest to hook the ball was very much a game within a game. After the match had concluded, no matter what the score believed by the other players to determine which team had won, the real winners would be the front row that had won more strikes against the head than the other. As a result, I've known matches where, despite one team having conceded at least sixty points without reply, whilst all their team-mates would sit in their changing room in some gloom, their front row could be all smiles if they'd taken more against the head, and be engaged in an animated, self-congratulatory conversation about their own undoubted, proven superiority. "What'd you mean, we lost the match? We didn't. You did. We won you prats more than enough possession; not our fault you buggered it up."

However, whilst the best prop forwards are undoubtedly intellectually elevated, I do have to confess that there are those that are perhaps a little less elevated than others. More years ago than I care to consider, there was one such individual called Nigel. A truly splendid physical specimen with enormous thighs and solid muscle and bone throughout, Nigel came into the senior game with a truly impressive pedigree – England U15, U16 and U17, England Colts, etc. However, the club's selection committee felt he was still a little too callow to be plunged straight into the club's first team as he was as yet unversed in what the media delights in calling the darker arts of the Front Row Union, like drinking a pint of aftershave and having a head-butting contest with a pillar box. In consequence, he was selected for the second team and given over to the tutelage of Ron, a huge and wonderfully erudite Welsh prop of immense charm and wit.

Ron was a semi-permanent fixture in the second team, his place there cemented by a mixture of talents. These included ownership of an early model of the ubiquitous Ford Transit van, into which ten players at a pinch could be crammed for an away game; a melodious, rolling bass-baritone voice that made even the filthiest of rugby songs seem not only acceptable but something of an art form; and a glass eye. To most people, playing rugby, especially in the front row, with a glass eye sounded like a major impediment if certainly not a risk too far, but Ron had turned it into a truly legendary asset. Resulting from a childhood accident, Ron had not only adjusted fully to this loss but had carefully calculated how it could be turned to his best advantage. For opposing props unaware of his wiles, their first game against Ron could be and often was a nightmare as he could slip his glass eye in and out of its socket apparently at will. Accordingly, at the first scrum where his team were under pressure, Ron would give out a great cry and sink to his knees, his hands over his eyes. The scrum would break up, the opposition front row in more than a little surprise, and Ron would then take his hands from his face and stare up at his opposite number, fixing him with an eyeless socket.

"I've lost my eye," he would proclaim dramatically, before pleading in a woebegone voice to the poor dupe opposite, "be careful not to tread on it, boyo."

This, of course, immediately caused the opposing front row to rear up and back with considerable alarm and dismay, lifting their feet and moving away with uncommon urgency. Ron, having previously palmed his glass eye when he'd covered his face with his hands, would then give out a roar of mixed relief and triumph, pretend to extract it from the mud where his opposing prop's feet had been and then, wiping it on a handkerchief from his shorts' pocket, he'd polish it and, with what his team-mates came to regard as an increasingly overly dramatic flourish, pop it back in its socket, to the generally slack-jawed consternation of the opposing team. After this experience, Ron's opposite number tended to be rather nervous about packing down against Ron, who'd gaily spend the rest of the afternoon grinding the poor sod into the ground.

Against opposition of sterner mettle or more experience, Ron was known to deliberately pop his eye out onto the churned ground between the two steaming packs of forwards, once they'd come together for a scrum. Even for those of us who'd seen this little trick before it could still be a little unnerving for Ron's eye to suddenly appear beneath you, staring vacantly upwards. In desperate defensive positions, such as their put-in under our posts, this ploy was almost guaranteed to gain you at least two yards, and a strike against the head was often thereby achieved. Indeed, Ron only ceased this practise when he fell out with the second-row forward behind him. Ron claimed that, when his eye had been thus ejected into the mud in the greater interest of the team, the second row player had deliberately stamped his eye into the ground, in the kind of malicious opportunism of which front-row forwards are all too aware second-row forwards are not only capable but prone.

Anyway, to return to Nigel's education in necromancy, after he and Ron had been playing together for a few weeks and Nigel had presumably become a little more aware of not only how the senior game was played but also some of the tricks of the trade, Nigel was seen to sidle up to Ron in the clubhouse bar one Saturday evening, after the afternoon's entertainment. Nigel looked a little embarrassed and, taking Ron slightly to one side and having looked around to ensure he wouldn't be overheard too easily, he stated, sotto voce, "Excuse me, Ron, I don't want to worry you, but there's something wrong with one of your eyes."

Ron slowly turned to face Nigel. "How'd you mean, boyo?"

Nigel hunkered closer to Ron. "Well, they're not always looking in the same direction, Ron; d'you think you should go and have them checked?"

Ron considered this for a moment. "Is one of them worse than the other, boyo?"

Nigel again looked around to ensure that nobody would share in Ron's forthcoming embarrassment. "The left one, Ron."

Ron gazed expressionlessly at Nigel for a moment, then plucked his left eye from its socket and showed it to Nigel. "This one, Nigel?" he enquired, and then proceeded to polish his eye on a large silk handkerchief that he always carried with him for such purpose before casually popping it back into his socket.

Nigel watched this bravura performance without any apparent surprise. When it was over he looked at Ron considering before asking, in a studiously nonchalant tone, "False, is it?"

As Ron later remarked, there was a moral in this story; don't try and be a clever clogs – someone could be keeping an eye out for you.

Being very much a larger than life figure, Ron never lost an opportunity to enhance his standing, especially in the eyes of the opposition, by judicious use of this ability to extract and re-insert his glass eye at will. This was mostly done after a match; well, he didn't want to give them prior warning of what he might do during the match, did he? Nevertheless, even if they'd been the victim of one of Ron's practices during the match, it could still be a little unnerving if you came up to Ron from behind, to buy him a beer or simply engage him in conversation, and he'd deliberately turn slowly to you showing an eyeless socket. It was bad enough for the men he'd played against; for their wives or girlfriends who hadn't yet been made aware of Ron's disability, it could be positively horrifying. You could always tell where Ron was in a clubhouse; if you couldn't see him, his position would be given away by the series of muffled shrieks that would occur as he was introduced to various unknowing females. Popping his glass eye back in its socket with his customary flourish of a brightly coloured silk handkerchief would also leave them open-mouthed.

Ron considerably enjoyed greeting members of the female sex in this way, especially as, having thus met him for the first time, their sensibilities would be so affected that, wherever they were whilst Ron was still present, their eyes and attention would be drawn back magnetically to him. Ron, of course, would play upon this regular, fascinated attention shamelessly, popping his glass eye out for them, winking over his empty eye-socket and then replacing his eye again. Whilst none of us were ever sure if he was taking the piss or not, Ron often claimed that losing his eye was the best thing that could have happened to him, at least as far as attracting women was concerned. Certainly, he was seldom unaccompanied by an attractive young lady, although I suspect that Ron's marvellously cheerful and gregarious character would have ensured that, anyway.

Ron's other regular little jest would be when, standing at the bar, he'd just been handed a fresh pint. Having taken a mouthful from it (and waiting until the surrounding attention was focussed on him), he'd whip out his glass eye and drop it into his glass before announcing that he needed to go for a piss. As often as I'd watched this act, seeing this pint of beer with Ron's glass eye on the bottom, apparently staring cold-bloodedly at you, could be a little off-putting. For those who'd never seen it before, it was rather more disconcerting.

Another prop with whom I had many a happy time, most especially off the field, was Brian, a very solid citizen who hailed, originally, from Lancashire. On the face of it, Brian appeared a very introspective individual, almost taciturn, but that was only because he had a fairly evil sense of humour that he chose not to disclose whilst the more maniacal of our team-mates were strutting their stuff. He had one particular party trick that never failed to totally astonish strangers and which, even after we, his companions, had watched for a number of times, continued to fascinate us.

Now, Brian would typically bring out this party trick when some stranger would have been boasting as to the speed at which he could drink a pint of beer. Generally after a noisy prelude, in which his supporters would both loudly proclaim such individual's incredible achievements and urge him to cast aside his apparent reticence to demonstrate his capability to drink a pint of beer in less than 4 seconds, Brian would make some disparaging or dismissive remark about such achievement. This, naturally, would be seized on immediately by the supporters of the local champion with shouts of such as, "I'd like to see you do better" and "Put your money where your mouth is."

This was exactly what Brian wanted and he'd carefully state, "I'll bet thee anything thee likes I can completely finish off pint of beer afore 'e can." Of course, this led to any number of bets taking place in a general furore and I can remember bets totalling well over £200 being laid; and that was over forty years ago. Two pints of beer would then be set up on a table with the two contestants facing one another from opposite sides. Then, before the contest began, Brian would carefully dig the pit into which he planned for his opponent to fall. "Reet," he'd say, "let's make sure that terms of bet are clearly understood and agreed by thee and me."

The local champion would look at Brian in slight puzzlement. This was just a simple race to see who could drink a pint of beer the fastest. "What?" he'd invariably reply.

"I'm betting thee cannot down glass of ale afore me," Brian would slowly state, rather pedantically in most on-lookers' eyes.

"Right! Yeah, right," his opponent would generally reply impatiently, and Brian would nod in satisfaction, as if to say, let battle commence.

Brian's adversary would then get into a kind of crouching position, one hand behind his back and the other extended, in a grasping manner, ready to grab the pint of beer nearest him the second the moment came. Brian, by comparison, would seem grossly unprepared for the contest, standing leisurely at ease, watching his opponent with a gentle anticipatory smile on his face.

When the publican, who would not have wholly willingly agreed to act as independent arbitrator, shouted "Go!" the acclaimed speedster would immediately grab the pint glass in front of him and, with an incredible display of rapid drinking, would pour almost all of the beer down his throat in but a few seconds before placing the pint glass, upside down, on top of his head. He had performed wondrously and, although a few rivulets of beer made their way down his face, his ear-to-ear grin would proclaim his certainty of victory, a result that his noisily congratulatory supporters would clearly feel was undeniably his. This would especially be the case when they looked across at Brian, who had usually drunk only about half his pint by then.

In his own time, and to derisory chants of "Loser, loser" from his opponents' friends and backers, Brian would drink his pint, place his empty glass upon his head to prove that he'd not left any beer un-drunk, and would then place the glass on the table in front of him. His opponent would then lean forward, right hand outstretched to shake Brian's whilst announcing, "Hard luck, mate; good try".

Carefully ignoring the proffered hand, Brian would look at his apparently successful opponent and say, "Why's that, lad, we're not finished yet." He'd then pick up his pint glass and give it a fairly sharp tap on the top of the table, breaking off a number of smallish pieces. Then to the absolutely eye-popping astonishment of just about everybody present, Brian would put one of the pieces of glass into his mouth and proceed to crunch it into tiny, more digestible portions. In what could only be described as a deafening silence, having swallowed this first mouthful, he'd then open his mouth wide and turn his head from side to side in proof that he hadn't somehow rid himself of the glass by a devious or magical trick and, picking up another piece of the broken glass, would perform the same exercise with that.

By now, the initial dumbfounded silence would have been broken by shouts of amazement, disbelief and, in some cases, of scarcely diluted apprehension. Brian would ignore all this with calm unconcern but, his opponent would stare at him unbelievingly. Brian would then really rub it in by leaning forward, pointing to the local hero's empty glass and saying, "C'mon, lad, eat oop; thee'll have to start soon if thee wants to win."

Not unnaturally, I never saw any opponent of Brian's in such a contest ever try to match him in consuming the glass as well, usually to the not inconsiderable relief of the publican. Others would be less enthusiastic. The individual concerned would often totter away, completely deflated by the abject trouncing he'd received, albeit admittedly out of left field. His supporters would also be substantially disgruntled, having seen what had seemed like easy money snatched away from them by what they evidently regarded as wholly unfair if not dastardly means, and some tried to welsh on their bets. Whilst this would generate heated arguments, the various bets would virtually always be honoured once memories were drawn back to Brian's carefully worded request for confirmation of the rules for winning the contest.

And how did Brian come to develop this astounding capability? He was born into a circus family, the son of a sword-swallower, or so he claimed. Just goes to show that, although there are indeed a number of big, mentally challenged and dubiously co-ordinated lumps lumbering around on rugby pitches, mostly in the second row, you never know what you're going to get from a member of the Front Row Union.

THE EXTRAORDINARY EXTRA B

When I went to my secondary school, Westcliff High School for Boys, I was excited but not nervous. Even though I'd suddenly been moved from my comfort zone, and the junior and primary school that I'd attended were no longer the totality of my horizon, my father had been to the same school before me and I'd often accompanied him when he'd gone there on Saturdays to use the school's changing facilities before playing rugby on nearby pitches. Thus, not only was the physical structure of my new school comparatively well known to me but I'd also been aware for some while that going there would be an immense and wonderful improvement on my junior school. There, the only facilities we had for games or outside exercise of any nature was on one small area between the junior and primary schools that was completely covered with tarmac. This was not because I'd attended an especially poorly provided junior school; all the local junior schools in the area that I can remember were similarly disadvantaged. In my new secondary school, we had numerous fields that provided rugby and cricket pitches, an athletics track and sundry grassy areas on which we could all run about, wrestle and generally do whatever we wanted. This was an exceptional improvement, as were the schools' buildings themselves, only having been built in the early 1920s. And a major aspect of my enjoyment was the amount of organised physical education to which we were all introduced.

Back in junior school, the only time we had organised games was once a year, in the summer, to select representatives for the school at the sports day held for all junior schools in the local district. That and the occasional game of rounders. Apart from that, all the exercise we received was the self-organised games of football played by up to about fifty a side in a playground which contemporaneously hosted about another hundred children for whatever they wanted to do in their breaks or lunch-hours and who stood or played whatever in the middle of the aforesaid game of football. So, for me, the incredible variety of sports available at my secondary school was uplifting in the extreme. Furthermore, because I had accompanied my father every Saturday to both his rugby games in winter and cricket matches in summer, I had a material advantage over the other boys who started that September. Additionally, my physical build has always tended towards the bulky or cuddly; not for me the elegant footwork and extravagant swerves and sidesteps of my slimmer, faster team-mates. In consequence, I was always destined to be a foot soldier in the trenches. And didn't just thoroughly enjoy but gloried in it.

Thus, when I left school in 1959, with some understanding of but also an undying, life-long love of rugby, I instantly joined my father's rugby club. There, like nearly all newcomers, especially the naive, unsuspecting innocents who'd just left school, my first few games were for the club's fifth team, the Extra B.

In those days, the Extra B was captained by Sid, who was a wonderfully affable, rotund gentleman with a moustache which never quite grew into a full Emperor Franz-Josef set. I don't think I ever knew exactly what Sid did for a living, but the skills and devilish cunning with which he gathered together his team every Saturday was legendary. What needs to be realised is that, unless Sid employed all kinds of devious and underhanded means, he would have very little say in the selection of the Extra B. Logically, one would expect that no actual carefully considered selection for, or choice between two or more players for any one position in the Extra B, would occur; Sid should simply have had to try and cobble together a team from the waifs and strays left over from the deliberations of the higher teams. And these players, one would assume, would be those that no-one else wanted to select; indeed, would probably not select at any price for whatever reasons. But, week after week, Sid would trot out onto the pitch on the Saturday with a team that often not only actually came close to numbering fifteen, but would probably have given the club's third team an extremely hard game. How so? Firstly, Sid took his position as captain of the Extra B and all its related duties and responsibilities very seriously. Being a man of immense subtlety, cunning flattery and a deep-seated knowledge, he played on the fact that what his players regarded as the most important event of the day was not the match itself but the extended shenanigans that would occur after the game. This was especially true as regards away matches, firstly in the oppositions' clubhouses and then in the innumerable pubs that he would know were on the route home (or close to, give or take a few miles). These away matches were thereby transmuted into foreign tours with the participants often only arriving back to their own clubhouse at no earlier than midnight. Although this meant that they then had to face the wrath of their female partners, a goodly number of them were fairly incapacitated by that time, so they hardly knew or cared which way was up. Thus it was not unusual to see a player, a mindless, beaming, eyes-closed smile adorning his face, being driven home by his incandescent, eyes-slitted, teeth-gritted partner. Retribution, sadly, and at a monumental level, would follow in the morning. But then the guilty, down-trodden and remorseful one would usually have another fortnight to gather together a host of brownie points before the next away fixture.

As a result, over the term of a number of seasons of Sid's captaincy, the Extra B had acquired a reputation, a charisma, far in excess of its seemingly lowly playing status. It had, in fact, become a club within a club. And this situation had been carefully nourished by Sid, by gathering around him a nucleus of old and cunning players, most of whom had once been highly competent; if not at playing rugby then certainly in drinking beer at incredible speed or at successfully performing numerous weird and wonderful after-match drinking games such as Cardinal Puff. By the time I joined the club, Sid's Extra B had gained enormous renown, and not just locally. Indeed, when my father, a close school friend of Sid's became aware that my first game for the club would be for the Extra B, he nodded thoughtfully and approvingly. My mother was far more uncertain; she was aware that the Extra B had been created in Sid's image and had also known him and his behavioural patterns for at least two decades. "Don't worry, darling," my father had assured her comfortingly, "he'll be in safe hands," adding, far more ambiguously, "he'll be taught a lot."

What my father didn't tell my mother was exactly what I'd be likely to be taught, and by what means. Or that I'd finish that first appearance for the Extra B leaning on the doorbell at nearly two o'clock in the morning. Nevertheless, despite her stern face and acid welcome home, I strongly suspect she was not in the slightest bit surprised; my mother was always the intelligent one in our family.

Additional to creating this almost self-perpetuating mafia, to boost the already over-inflated egos of its members, Sid constructed and maintained an information-gathering network of which MI5 would have been extremely envious. This enabled Sid, nearly week after week, to delight his regulars with the appearance amongst them of guest stars. Thus, when Sid discovered that a first team player returning from injury was looking for a run-out lower down, Sid would squirrel away this information after gaining that worthy's un-retractable agreement to appear in the Extra B, probably signed in his own blood. Then, although the various captains were supposed to be honour bound at the Monday night selection committee meeting to advise of any unexpected player availability, Sid would sit there keeping stumm and maintaining his gently smiling expression. Whilst the subsequent, unexpected victory of the Extra B due to the heroic efforts of the returning first team player would result in indignant shouts from the captains of the higher teams, Sid would just shrug his shoulders and smile blandly.

But if this carefully contrived bolstering of the Extra B's resources pissed off Sid's peers, that was as nothing to the howls of envy when he surreptitiously captured the services of a rugby player of some renown who was a friend or relative of another club member and had become very temporarily resident in the area.

Probably the best example of this was when Stephen, a scrumhalf who ordinarily played for a highly regarded team in Scotland, if I remember rightly, and had been capped two or three times by his country, came down to attend the wedding of a cousin living locally. However Sid discovered Stephen's availability and pedigree was never discovered. Suffice to say, on the Saturday, Sid turned up with Stephen for a match against some pretty stern opposition which the rest of the Extra B were not that optimistic they could win. By half-time, all such doubts had been dissipated as they were 20-0 up, all the points having been scored by Stephen, with four tries and four conversions (in those days, a try was only worth 3 points). Apparently, his degree of superiority was so marked that, after the manner in which he'd scored his first two tries, the visiting team literally gave up trying to tackle or chase him and simply walked back disconsolately to line up behind their own posts every time he started off on a run with the ball.

In the second half, clearly Stephen must have become bored because, instead of sprinting and side-stepping his way at speed through the semi-static and utterly bemused players in the opposition, employing literally stunning hand-offs to further deter attempted tackles, he generously tried to get his new team-mates on the scoreboard. Unfortunately, as laudable an ambition as this was, it had a number of serious flaws, the principal one being that Stephen, to misquote Bobby Jones, played a game of rugby with which none of his new team-mates was familiar. Thus, instead of dancing off with the ball as it emerged from a scrum, maul, ruck or lineout, Stephen began passing it out and principally to his flyhalf, Alan, a long-term, fully paid-up member of the Extra B mafia.

What modern players have to realise at this point is that the rugby ball we played with then, especially in the lower teams of smaller clubs, was nothing like what they are used to now. Any similarities between the two can only be described as purely co-incidental. These days, it has no bladder inside and is made of a synthetic, water-proof material, with a dimpled pattern all over to enable it to be caught and retained more easily. Before 1980, by comparison, rugby balls consisted of four leather panels stitched together with a rubber bladder inside. The problem with these balls was that it was not that easy to hold them securely. When they were new they were a lovely tan colour and shaped in a true oval. They were also very shiny and, even in the dry opening and closing months of the rugby season, pretty slippery. Come the dark months of winter and the rain, sleet and snow, they became almost impossible to hold, particularly if you'd been stuck on the wing all game and had not just numb but frozen hands. This made the try that Andy Hancock scored for England against Scotland at Twickenham in 1965, to win that Calcutta Cup match even more remarkable; I was in the South Stand, almost behind the posts, when Andy received a pass from Mike Weston well within his own 25 before evading at least two tackles to run the length of the field to score in the dying minutes of the game. And that was the be all and end all of my memories of that match; it had been a bloody awful game, played in pissing rain almost throughout. And as Andy told me some years later when we combined to provide coaching to a selection of under 20s, he'd had hardly a pass all afternoon before that, and he was more terrified that, with hardly any feeling in his hands, he'd drop the ball than anything else.

But if the leather balls the better teams were given to play with were almost a total lottery, those that arrived down in teams like the Extra B would have been viewed with horrified astonishment if not incredulity by most players of any renown. In many of the small rugby clubs I've known, a fresh supply of balls was acquired for the beginning of each new season. These, after each had been used for ten or twelve weeks, would percolate down to their second team. At the same time, the previous season's new balls were gradually passed down to the third team; and so on. This meant that the newest of the rugby balls that the Extra B ever got to play with was four years old and, because in the intervening years some balls used by the higher teams had been lost or gone walkabout in any way, many of the balls used in Extra B games could be many years older still.

Therefore, when one turned out for the Extra B, the captain would bring along with him, additional to his kit and a bag of sliced lemons, oranges or grapefruit, a beaten-up, muddy, ex-military kitbag containing up to about six balls. You'll notice I've not described them as being either rugby or oval. Why not? Well, rugby balls should be, by definition, oval but that was the last shape anyone could ascribe to these balls. Once they might have been, and a delightful tan in colour, with a feel and a smell of a new horse saddle. Now, however, they were a strange, ugly shape best described as rhomboidal, and almost universally black. Furthermore, even if not used for weeks, they had been deployed so often in thick mud and heavy rain that they had come to retain a somewhat unctuous, slimy patina, not unlike what one imagined it might feel like if you had to pick up a large dog's faeces. Also, after so many years of use on pitches liberally be-spotted with seagull shit, they had a distinct and wholly disagreeable aroma, too. Finally, after all these years of a perpetually downwards decline, these balls had become bloated and considerably heavier with misuse and lack of hygiene; pretty similar to some of the more elderly players, come to think of it.

So, when Alan received his first pass from Stephen he was considerably surprised in more ways than one. Firstly, it came straight to him and at a catchable height. Normally, a scrumhalf in the Extra B had neither the energy nor strength to pass one of these deformed medicine balls anywhere really close to his flyhalf. Because the pass was so slow, the flyhalf would stand much closer to his scrumhalf than you'll ever see in higher class rugby but, even then, its direction would be anyone's guess. It could be down by the flyhalf's ankles, be thrown in a slow parabola to land just behind his ear, be chucked about two yards in front of him or could come trundling slowly along the ground towards him, end over end, pursued with ever-increasing hunger and optimism by a host of ravenous, predatory forwards, including some of his own.

Alan's second surprise was that the ball not only came straight at him but at rocket pace, bursting straight through his limp hands and, thumping into his stomach at muzzle velocity, knocked both the wind out of his lungs and him sideways off his feet. As clearly distressed by the physical pain and shock he'd suffered, it was later rumoured that what upset Alan most was that he'd been hammered into just about the deepest and most foul-smelling puddle on the pitch, which meant he'd have to get his kit washed before the next game; not an action that figured in his normal game plan.

A not inconsiderable delay then resulted. These days, it would probably be for a similar period because of the admirable concern about player health and safety that exists throughout the game and the resultant availability of good medical treatment at nearly all levels. Then, the only medical accoutrements we had were a bucket of cold water and the magic sponge. Since, at an Extra B fixture, normally played out somewhere not in the known universe where one man and his dog would be a record crowd, trained medical support was rare indeed, unless one of the players was a doctor. Typically, one of the injured player's team-mates would pick the magic sponge out of the bucket, dripping with icy water, and apply it wholly dispassionately to the back of the injured player's neck or, pulling back his shorts and jock-strap, to his testicles. What the medical justification for this latter application was I never knew, but I also never knew it fail. The recipient, wherever injured and to whatever extent, would jerk upright with an open-mouthed, wide-eyed shudder, bound to his feet and stand shivering there, dog-like, until he came to his senses and generally limped off to whatever he might have believed was his normal position. Curiously, one of the few times that I experienced an untold wealth of medical advice being available at the occurrence of such an injury was in a match against St. Mary's Hospital. However, this turned out to be worse than ever as the bloody medical students could agree amongst themselves neither the exact nature of the injury, nor what should best be done about it.

Anyway, Alan was far too wily and experienced a bird to lie there waiting for this coup de grace to be applied, a very wise decision given the suspected psychotic instincts of some of his team-mates, and struggled to his feet with an ashen complex after only a few minutes of lying on the floor rasping stentoriously. Even so, the match could not be re-started immediately as about half-a-dozen of the players had ambled off the pitch to have a restorative fag, and refused to return until they'd smoked them.

Whilst this extended delay occurred, Alan got together with Stephen to educate the latter in the ways of the real world and, at the next scrum, stood a good ten yards further away than normal. Even with that precaution and with Stephen considerably lowering the speed of his pass to below terminal velocity, Alan only just held onto the ball. Ironically, Alan was so pleased with his achievement that he ran straight into his opposite number, a physical element of rugby that virtually all flyhalves will evade at all costs, and dropped the ball.

After the match in which, despite all Stephen's able promptings, only one more try was scored (by Stephen), Alan was subsequently asked what it was like to play with an international scrumhalf. "Fucking terrifying," was his immediate heart-felt answer.

"What?" said one of his listeners, "even after you and he had that conversation when you fell over?"

"I didn't fall over," returned Alan, rather frostily. "I was knocked arse over tit by his pass."

"OK," acknowledged his questioner, a winger in the Extra B who'd probably not received a pass from Alan in over three years, "but what was it like to receive his passes after that?"

Alan considered a second then replied, succinctly, "Like being hit in the chest by an elephant's turd at 100 miles an hour." Mind you, it was noticeable how much his previously loudly declared criticism of and disdain for flyhalves appearing in internationals declined after that.

Another reason for the consummate ease with which Sid managed to gather around him a devoted gaggle of players was the fact that a number of them were what are euphemistically described as "characters". These are individuals who, if you had observed in the street or at a normal party the kind of behaviour they were wont to display at rugby matches, both on and off the pitches, you would label as highly eccentric, as lunatics or even as downright hooligans. And you wouldn't be wrong. In addition, and far more acceptable, were those players whose physical deterioration and lack of eye-hand co-ordination had forced them to accept these disabilities and concentrate, instead, on their off-field expertise, usually involving the consumption of not inconsiderable amounts of alcohol. Or was it, perhaps, the other way around? Anyway, Barry was one of those latter regulars of the Extra B.

Nearly eight years older than me, Barry was already a well-established character by the time I joined the Old Boys. Possessed of a singularly un-co-ordinated body, I never knew Barry to play anywhere except on the wing. Even if we turned up with only thirteen men and the two missing were both centres, Barry would not be asked to replace one of the missing players; by unanimous comment consent he was instructed to remain out on the wing. It was just as well. Barry was so inept at catching a ball that it had long been recognised that there was little if any point in passing it to him. On one renowned occasion, for example, with no alternative, one of his team-mates gave a perfect pass to Barry, at a decent pace between chest and stomach, and slightly in front of him so Barry could run onto it. Barry watched it coming and then made a perfect hoop with his arms through which the ball passed dead centre and then into touch.

That was probably when Barry was at his best, when the ball was in touch. He had learned, very early on, I'm told, of the value of delaying the throw-in at a line-out. With the more elderly players gasping for air, or a fag, or both, even thirty seconds stood with hands on knees wondering why the fuck they were still doing this was truly a lifeline. Barry soon cottoned onto this and had an innovative number of means for failing to quickly bring the ball back from wherever it had gone or from where he had inadvertently or surreptitiously kicked it. In turn, this meant that Sid had no need to call too often upon his other ploy to gain a critically needed respite for burning lungs and failing knees. This was to call upon Geoff, a bulky prop of immense experience, to perform his well-known dying swan act. One trouble with that was Geoff would enter far too readily into the spirit of the thing and I know of at least one referee who wanted to stop the game and have someone run to a nearby house to call for an ambulance. Only thing that Geoff really suffered from was acute over-acting, and even the dumbest referee would start having suspicions if Geoff keeled over and rolled around on the ground in un-melodious agony more than twice in a match. Especially if, having received Sid's nod, he climbed miraculously to his feet with shaky heroism. Too much of that and we'd have seen more coaches than Lourdes.

Barry's more subtle and home-grown delaying tactics were much more credible, and he took just as seriously the rest of his throwing-in duties. Remember, back then, it was not the hookers but the wings that threw the ball into the line-out. Good thing, too, the poor sods would often have frozen to death, otherwise. Barry could therefore be relied upon to take appropriate defensive action if we were losing our own line-outs. A couple of words from Sid and, at the next line-out, none of us would jump and either their player at the front would be rendered semi-conscious by a cannonball throw from Barry to the back of his head or their jumper would be severely disinclined to jump any more by a ball hurled with similar explosive speed into his testicles. Barry was always the perfect gentleman when these unfortunate accidents occurred, apologising profusely to all concerned, shaking his head with concern and remorsefully stating he didn't know how it had happened; it had sort of slipped from his hand. No recriminatory reaction ever came from the opposing team but they got the message; afterwards, we were allowed to jump for the ball at our own line-outs without opposition.

Nevertheless, for all these failings in skill, Barry did provide us with one magical moment that none of us who were there will ever forget. You know when the truly great performers, like Gerald Davies, David Duckham, Phil Bennett and Jason Robinson get the ball in their hands and conjure up something totally extraordinary out of nothing and you hear a collective gasp of awe, astonishment and pure wonder from the crowd? Well, to be honest, it was nothing like that but, judged against Barry's standard level of play, one might say it was his Ephesus moment.

Somehow, and nobody who was there can ever remember exactly how, so overwhelming was the memory of what followed, Barry got the ball in his hands. We were playing on the normal pitch used by the Extra B when at home; a pitch on a slightly forlorn public park on the edge of a council housing estate built when architects were failed pill-box designers. Not only quite close to the sea but relatively high up, this park was generally carefully ignored by everyone during the week except by large gatherings of particularly anti-social seagulls. These birds would swarm up from the Thames Estuary and empty their bowels systematically over the two pitches there. If anyone in Bomber Command still has any interest in the tactical use of carpet bombing, I'd strongly recommend they observe the flying patterns of these birds and the manner in which, despite both pitches being lined by trees and asphalt paths on either side, the guano never landed on anything except the two pitches.

Thus, when visiting teams came to play the Extra B on this pitch (or the Extra A, on that adjacent), those who'd never played there before would come and stare at its state with concerned amazement. To their often unkind comments and demands as to how they could be expected to play there we'd merely smile sympathetically and shrug our shoulders, whilst their team-mates who'd previously undergone this experience looked on with resigned countenances.

Late during one such then scoreless game, in deep, dark midwinter, when the pitch was especially nasty, with its surface bearing a generous, viscous mix of mud and bird shit by then sickeningly churned up into a real witches' brew, Barry found himself, out by the touch-line, with the ball in his hands. Even more likely to induce panic in the Barry that we thought we knew was the fact that his opposite number, an unusually big, burly and athletic lad for teams as lowly as this, was rushing towards him with obvious menace. Incredibly, not only did Barry not panic at this almost certainly unique experience for him, but he executed a move of such skill and daring that, afterwards, even the visiting team applauded him without reserve, like a modern day Horatius. And even the ranks of Tuscany could scarce forbear a cheer, indeed.

For what did Barry do? Realising that, unless he did something dramatic, he would probably suffer some form of dismemberment, he kicked the ball ahead and over the top of his onrushing opponent. Actually successfully kicking the ball was an achievement in itself for Barry; typically, if he tried to do so, he'd drop it down to where his feet should be only for his kicking foot to completely miss the ball. This time, however, he came up trumps and not only connected with the ball but sent it soaring perfectly towards the opponents' try-line, some sixty yards or so ahead. So what, I hear you say, what's so fantastic about that? Well, having brushed past his now disarmed opposite number desperately trying to put on the brakes and turn around, Barry not only had to run over sixty yards to catch up with the ball but do so in conditions akin to the trenches in World War 1. And all the rest of us, in both teams, suddenly realised this would not, in these conditions, be a sprint but a marathon, with the probable scoring of a winning try the prize to he who could drag himself across the pitch to the ball's possible final destination. As this realisation set in, all the remaining players, plus the referee, turned nearly as one and, struggling to lift tired limbs out of the noxious glue beneath us, strove to get there first. But Barry brought out the ace of trumps. Skipping smartly to one side, off the pitch, he ran up the pristine asphalt path that ran alongside the pitch the entire sixty yards or so. Then, almost exactly contemporaneously with the ball losing the last of its forward momentum and slowing, seemingly in slow motion to the rest of us, to a stop just over the try-line, Barry leaped back onto the pitch and threw himself forward onto the ball to score the game-winning and never-to-be-forgotten try.

I can't remember if Barry ever scored another try. He might well have done but, somehow, I doubt it. Not that it matters; this was an extraordinary try, appropriately scored for that extraordinary Extra B.

THE FOLLIES OF YOUTH

W hen I first left school, back in 1959, it wasn't getting a job as an articled clerk with a firm of local chartered accountants that filled me with anticipation or enthusiasm, it was joining the Old Boys rugby club.

In the fourth year of my grammar school, by comparison with today's far more extensive efforts, comparatively little was done to discover what innate talents we might have so as to help identify suitable employment once we left school. Such efforts as were made were often to persuade us to stay on at school and enter the sixth form before moving on from there to university. Indeed, when those of us who'd spent the first four years in the A stream and were thus pushed into taking at least two O levels a year early but then declined the enthusiastic encouragement of our headmaster to take this route to higher education, we were treated with grave opprobrium. This, we believed, was due to a strong rumour that "The Boot", our much feared yet revered headmaster, the ugliest man in Christendom, a beautifully spoken and mannered man whose lips made Mick Jagger look thin-lipped, stood to receive an extra one pound a head for every pupil that entered university.

Certainly, the consequences of the decision of those of us who, for whatever reason, had opted not to progress to the sixth form were not slow in coming. Contemporaneously with the receipt of our results of taking Maths and English a year early came the notification that those of us with the gall to decide against university education had been demoted from A stream status in the fourth year to that of the C stream in the fifth, despite passing both O level exams.

You have to remember that, back then in the late 1950s, the percentage of school pupils in the UK that went on to university was only just over 20% and, whilst I never knew nor asked why my best friend, Tony, had no interest in following this road, my own decision was actually that of my parents. Thus being demoted to 5C carried neither stigma nor unhappiness for either of us as it reduced the number of lessons we had to attend per week from 40 to just 26, which meant we were freed up for 14 lessons a week. For Tony and me this was no penal sanction as it meant we could either utilise such free time to swot up on the other subjects on which we'd be tested in that year's O level exams (and which we actually did, from time to time) or on our more preferred activity of extra games.

In that memorably sunny summer of 1959, since there were nearly thirty of us who had either been similarly set aside or were sixth formers who had "excess study" periods of their own, we therefore enjoyed a wondrously care-free life, with our involvement in cricket and/or athletics being a key and integral element of each day's activities.

Sadly, I have now to confess it's probably true that such a lazy, relaxed period of my life inclined me towards a hedonistic life-style. So, having neither any real idea of what I wanted to do after leaving school or what occupation would be suitable for me, I was happy to accompany my father when he took me to visit a former school friend of his who was the senior partner in a small yet successful local firm of chartered accountants. There, in an office by my untutored eyes of fairly impressive status, I first met the man who was to be my principal over the next five years. He was a bronzed, handsome man in a beautifully cut suit with what seemed a welcome and, for me, quite surprising sense of humour. He was also concise and to the point and, having pointed out to me with calm but forceful assurance that, if I cared to check up on the Board of Directors of any public company of note, the most common qualification of its members would be that of a member of the Institute of Chartered Accountants in England & Wales, I was sold.

Unfortunately, it wasn't until later that it became clear to me that becoming both a member of the ICAEW and a director of a public company was not something that automatically followed signing articles. To my chagrin, and to my principal's well voiced irritation,

I was actually required to not only study but also pass examinations. This presented me with rather a problem, as I had already committed most of my spare time to playing Rugby Union; training on Tuesdays and Thursdays, plus playing in games on Saturdays and Sundays. Furthermore, as I grew older and more proficient at rugby, there was training for Rugby Sevens on Sunday mornings and representative matches on Wednesdays – firstly for Essex and then for the Eastern Counties. How could I possibly keep up with my studies when I had all these other responsibilities?

As a result, I fell further and further behind with my studies to be accepted as a member of the ICAEW. However, given the success and enjoyment I was deriving from my social activities, how could this possibly matter? This assessment as to what were the truly important things in life was confirmed by my first visit to Paris in February 1960. Ostensibly, this was for the purpose of watching France play England at rugby at Colombes on the Saturday and then, on the Sunday, to play for the Old Boys against the world-famous Racing Club de France, also at Colombes. Not on the same pitch, mind, but on some lesser terrain out the back of beyond.

On the Friday evening we flew out from Southend Airport to either Orly or Le Bourget (I can't remember which) on a somewhat decrepit Channel Airways Viscount. I can remember very little of that night apart from the fact that we meandered from bar to bar, mostly in and around Pigalle. Being, at 17, by far the youngest member of the group, I can now appreciate that the older members (and especially those who had been at school with my father) went considerably out of the way to keep me safe, especially when I was being sorely tempted by young, not-so-young and frankly middle-aged ladies wishing to introduce me to the delights of Paris, whatever those might have been; I certainly can't remember any of that, either.

Saturday went pretty well; at least as far as the international was concerned. Much to our relief and to the apparent disgust and loudly expressed fury and contempt of the French fans, the result was a 3-3 draw. Afterwards, filing out into the comparatively bleak and inhospitable areas with which Colombes was surrounded, all thoughts were on getting back to the City of Light and its world-renowned attractions, hopefully mostly illicit. Packed tight into old Metro trains, we all began looking forward, with improbable and almost certainly unachievable ambitions, to a night out in Paris.

The trip back became more and more good-tempered and friendly as the rival groups of supporters shared bottles of cognac and scotch and toasted "la concorde". So, by the time we all fell out of our carriages at succeeding Metro hubs, we resembled nothing so much as turkeys ready for plucking at the doors of the myriads of nightclubs that eagerly awaited us. To them, it must have seemed like Christmas.

Whichever night clubs we visited are lost in the nebulous fogs of time but I do recall, at about 2 o'clock in the morning, a gang of about eight of us finished up at Les Halles, what was then the marvellous but incredibly superior equivalent of what was then Covent Garden. It was an extraordinary pot pourri of humanity. You had the hard-working and rather caustic workers in their bleu de travail, pushing laden and unladen trollies to and from the camions impatient to deliver the fresh vegetables and fruit to their waiting marchands de légumes across Ile de France; the happy drunks, French and English, from the rugby international, often inconveniently blocking the ways of such trollies, beamingly looking to end their night with a decent hot meal at one of the seemingly inexhaustible number of enticingly attractive restaurants that both surrounded and extended the district; and, lastly, there were the beautifully dressed élites of Parisian society, just out of L'Opéra, with the men in dinner suites or tails and the ladies in ball gowns with fur stoles and the like, seeking a late night-cap and, thereafter, no doubt some other warming activity.

Even nearly sixty years later I can still conjure up those never-to-be forgotten images with little effort, and it invariably brings a smile to my lips and a warmth to my heart, and I find myself nodding conspiratorially with my ghosts of yesteryear.

Amongst our number was Malcolm, an exceedingly good player who had recently injured his leg and, whilst this would prevent him playing for us on this visit to Paris, his value to the rest of us was far more extensive than that. At the time, Malcolm was actually resident and working in Paris and it was he that had set up the match and booked our hotel, etc. Not only that but he now guided us to a restaurant I was to return to over the years on many occasions, Au Chien Qui Fume, an unrivalled brasserie with a suitably iconic sign hanging outside of a Scotch Terrier smoking a Meerschaum Pipe.

Still located at 33 Rue du Pont Neuf, Au Chien Qui Fume was heaving that night with crowds of would-be diners vigorously contending to be the next to enter. Malcolm, however, had done his homework and, having previously not just booked two tables but lubricated the palms of the doormen, together with their forceful help, he miraculously whisked us through the baying crowd.

Inside, it was all I had expected it to be – Renoir and Toulouse-Lautrec would have recognised it instantly. Every table was not just full but had additional chairs jammed around it; the bar was seething, 3 or 4 deep, with diners quaffing various drinks and conversing loudly while waiting for the table they'd booked to become vacant. There were waiters everywhere, dressed in a uniform ensemble of black and white. All of them wore white shirts with black bow ties; black trousers, waistcoats and shoes with long white aprons down to well below their knees. Without exception (at least in my memory), they all balanced large trays on one outspread palm at shoulder-height or higher, using their other arm to divide the shouting, smoking, drinking mob to enable them to deliver their orders to the waiting recipients. And over all this bubbling, swaying heaving mass hung the scents I now always associate with Paris, even though it has diminished considerably over the years; the pungent aroma of black tobacco, of Gauloises and Gitanes; the almost sickly fumes of Ricard, Pernod and other pastis; and the all-enveloping cloak of garlic.

When we had finally struggled through all this to our two small tables and had shouted our order for 8 beers to a passing waiter who briefly nodded his acknowledgement before plunging immediately out of sight into the surrounding bodies, we looked around us in vain for a menu of any kind. Casting glances at the tables around us (those we could actually see); all their occupants appeared to have large bowls of some indistinguishable offering in front of them. Almost completely bewildered at all this, I turned to Malcolm seated beside me and shouted a question into his ear. "What can we get to eat here? What d'you recommend?"

Malcolm grinned and bellowed back at me, "Onion soup!"

Onion soup? That's not what I had been looking forward to. "No, thanks, I'd much rather have a steak au poivre!" I yelled in his ear.

Malcolm shook his head at the ignorance of this young tyro. "No, lad. At this time in the morning and with this crowd the only thing they'll serve is onion soup!"

I stared at him in perplexity. "But I don't want onion soup," I shouted.

"Suit yourself," Malcolm replied, shrugging his shoulders, "but, truly, it's all you'll get now and, believe me, it's a meal in itself – you won't want anything else."

A little dispirited, I shrugged my shoulders in defeat but, when the 8 enormous bowls were finally delivered to our tables, together with two even bigger bowls of immensely appetising French bread cut into fist-sized chunks, I was forced into a rapid reappraisal, much to Malcolm's satisfied amusement. Each bowl held a good deal in excess of a pint of thick onion soup although this was initially totally invisible. On top of the soup, as soon became apparent when trying to dip one's spoon into it, was a crust of large croutons covered with melted cheese. And it wasn't just a sprinkling of cheese shavings either. When you did managed to reach the soup and bring the spoon full of onions to your mouth, it came up dripping with long strings of molten cheese, almost like capellini. As unexpectedly delicious and filling as this dish proved to be, it also had its drawbacks, especially for a messy eater like me, as I later found I'd managed to decorate my shirt and jacket pretty liberally with these cheese strings.

After Au Chien Qui Fume I very vaguely recall being shepherded back along the streets of Paris, but no more than that.

Next morning, when I woke, although I was still fully clothed I was in a strange bed. I don't mean it wasn't my bed at home, but it also wasn't the hotel bed I'd slept in the previous night, either. Then, when I raised my head, I found I wasn't alone, either on the bed or in the room. I was sharing the bed, head to toe, with two others of my team-mates, and the other bed was likewise occupied. Not only that but, in the narrow space between the two beds, were two other somnolent bodies, all fully dressed.

I lowered my head again to try and think my way through this conundrum; was this some kind of Kafkaesque hallucination? And then I received proof positive of its actuality – the body lying next to me stirred slightly so as to position itself more comfortably and then gave out a lengthy, reverberating fart. However, although as lacking in sound as it was, its aroma more than made up for this. My own, disgusted vocal objection was fairly immediate but, as its insidious fingers of internal decay spread unopposed across the room, more and more groans and then protests were made. These were quickly followed by increasingly vociferous demands to know who was responsible for such revolting, anti-social behaviour. Of course, all 8 present denied they were in any way responsible and, although I knew full well who it was, I decided that discretion was the better part of valour seeing as the guilty one had been our club captain, lying on the bed beside me.

Alternatively, I suppose, it might be argued that the noxious fumes I had breathed in had had some kind of impact on my brain; something certainly had and it surely couldn't have been the non-stop alcohol consumption that I'd been forced to consume the previous night. Or might it have been, if only just a little? In any event, the rest of that morning and a good deal of the following afternoon can best be described as hazy. The only thing I do remember is what was virtually the last quarter of our game at Colombes against a junior team from Racing Club de France.

We had been looking forward to this match for some while as, in those days, Racing Club de France were very much a glamour team. Although I had yet to play against any French team at that stage, all the hard men, the really rough and nasty frogs were reputed to play for teams in the South of France; teams like Narbonne's, Pau, Montpellier, Toulon and Bayonne, etc. Racing Club de France, by comparison, were viewed as the metropolitan elite. On one famous occasion, they not only turned up for but played in the final of the French championship wearing bow ties, and drinking champagne in crystal flutes at half-time. Sadly, on a cold, windy day out on the barren plains of Colombes, the lower team that opposed us had no time for what they presumably regarded as the pretentious nonsense of their superiors and were only interested in laying into us with not untypical French zest.

Could I describe the game itself? Not really. I have hazy recollections of running around without either direction or any real effect right until the time I had to leave the field to vomit a copious amount of what vaguely resembled onions and cheese but smelt disgustingly like neither. I was not alone in taking this remedial action and such clearances of our innards certainly had an almost invigorating effect on our players. Instead of slowly lurching aimlessly around the field and desperately keeping at bay a pack of rampant frogs, we began to take the initiative. Up until then, the frogs had only failed to score because, firstly, they ostensibly wanted to inflict as much severe physical damage and pain as possible on the visiting rosbifs and, secondly, their level of skills was almost as non-existent as our own. But, re-energised as many of us had thus become, the tables had turned, combined with the last ebbing away of the home side's energies. In fact it was I, standing away on one wing, totally out of position whilst trying to draw breath into heaving lungs, to which one of the defenders mis-directed an aimless kick. Miraculously managing to hold on to the ball as it bounced, almost in slow motion towards me, I had only to lumber about thirty metres to score, unopposed, what turned out to be the only and winning try, with not a frog within any sort of distance around me.

Afterwards, I only remember being taken to the truly magnificent clubhouse of Racing Club de France in Rue de Saussure, on the edge of Bois de Boulogne. Accustomed as I was, first as a schoolboy and then as a very young adult to clubhouses of all the sports in which I participated, rugby, cricket and athletics, being ramshackle old buildings with little to recommend them, even though they were fondly supported and maintained, I was completely over-awed by the stupendous facilities of Racing. On our way to what, from my then very limited, provincial experiences could only be described as a banqueting hall, we were taken through at least two trophy rooms lined wall to wall, ceiling to floor, with enormous trophy cabinets, boasting collections of silverware that seemed at least as twice as extensive as our Queen's crown jewels, from every one of the many sports in which Racing is involved. Indeed, part of our extended trek to the celebratory festivities laid on by our hosts took us along a corridor that overlooked at least 6 indoor tennis courts, all being enthusiastically employed; philistine as I then was, I hadn't even realised there were indoor tennis courts.

Thus, when I returned home, I had experienced much that I had never even conceived before. Surely, therefore, I was no longer a boy but a fully-fledged adult, fully of worldly knowledge and wisdom?

Much to my chagrin, I was soon to discover that no-one else shared this concept. Certainly not my parents and most particularly not my employers, who soon disabused me, in spades, of all and any such lofty self-beliefs. Nevertheless, with ongoing wholly immature reasoning, I clung secretly to these nonsensical pretentions and continued, for some years to come, to spend as much of my evenings and weekends as possible in pursuing my rugby interests rather than my career in accountancy.

With such a childish bias also went a generally immature attitude to life and to social behaviour in particular. Of course, being amongst a number of similarly minded buffoons only exacerbated and extended my behaviour. There was, for example, the period when, at regular intervals, the younger, would-be macho bulls of the rugby club would hold and publicly announce the winner of the "Ugly Bird of the Month Contest". As you'll appreciate, this was a very popular and well-attended event, full of subtle elegance, although not all the jury's choices were universally applauded. What brought the entire structure crashing down though was the time when little Johnny announced the winner one evening in a packed pub; a pub not only packed with the critical and discerning followers of this great sport but also the young lady who was declared to be the ugliest one, together with a party of her followers.

For reasons unknown, she failed to detect the exquisite humour of the situation but was temporarily distracted by little Johnny's follow-up comment that, indeed, "she was the ultimate paper bag job." Not understanding what he meant, she turned to her friends and, being advised that Johnny was opining she was so ugly that she needed a paper bag over her head before any male would look at her, she picked up a pint glass from the bar and just about brained little Johnny with it. Happily, it was almost empty at the time so no drastic wastage occurred but we did lose much drinking time whilst we argued who should take Johnny to hospital and then in taking him to Accident & Emergency. There, whilst we shuffled around in increasing irritation, they stitched up little Johnny and we rushed back to the pub, desperate to get in a last pint or so before they closed.

That pub did not prove to be a happy hunting ground as regards persuading unaccompanied females to come home with us, for coffee and whatever else they could be persuaded to agree to. I remember one occasion when we met up with three of such young ladies and, after not inconsiderable effort, managed to get them to accompany us, all jammed into my less than commodious Mini, back to little Johnny's house, his parents being away for the weekend. The young lady I had decided was suitable for my attentions was a little plumpish and had a vivacious face, but wore a truly badly-cut coat. Indeed. I wondered why she hadn't been snapped up earlier in the evening by one of the greasy Lotharios who haunted that particular pub.

Then she took off her coat and I realised it was not badly cut at all. In fact, it had been superbly tailored; it was she that had the strange curves and lumps. Fortunately, her only immediate pressing desire was for a coffee and she soon made it clear she had no interest whatsoever in sharing her unique bodily dimensions with anyone, especially me. That was some relief but she soon grew bored of my less than whole-hearted attempts at conversation as it became readily apparent that her sole topic was the composition and goings-on of various Pop Bands, about which I knew bugger all and cared even less.

What I then considered to be perfectly normal attitudes and behavioural patterns not only remained with me for long years after I had departed childhood but, looking back now, it is obvious that I revelled and even gloried in them, far longer than almost all my peers did. Most of them had married and largely settled down in their early twenties and, thereafter, only escaped from their domestic bliss on odd occasions. Of course, when they did, and returned home decidedly the worse for wear, there were inevitable tongue-lashings, penalties and periods of stony silences they had to suffer from their wives (and in-laws) and, not really unnaturally, I was usually viewed as the disgraceful miscreant that had tempted these poor, gullible souls from the straight and narrow. But did this well-advertised distaste for my antics dismay me? Not on your life; I carried on my merry way for a great deal longer than my wife later told me caustically I should have done. This resulted in levels of strife for my friends with their wives and in-laws for some time yet to come and, although my attendance at the weddings of my younger friends was generally argued through, my greeting by my hosts, the parents of the bride, was almost certainly going to be tight-lipped and lacking in warmth. Did I care? Not in the slightest; how could I be upset with them when I was about to get royally pissed at their expense?

And thus my life rolled on until I was nearly thirty. But then arrived my come-uppance. I met, fell in love with and married Susie. If that, in itself, wasn't enough to bring a jerk on the reins, I also suffered a nasty eye injury playing rugby that, given the prognostications handed me by Moorfields, forced me to truly evaluate my new circumstances. I therefore decided to retire from playing rugby and, instead, concentrate on my marriage and on passing my exams to become a Chartered Accountant and, thereafter, expend the efforts and drive I'd previously reserved pretty much solely for rugby in developing a genuine career.

My parents considered this apparent transformation with substantial relief, albeit tinged with irritation it had taken me so long to grow up. Since they also felt that much of the credit for this having occurred was due to Susie, she was greeted with open arms. However, what they only discovered later was that Susie had a wild, impetuous streak of her own that was to lead both her and me into other bizarre and note-worthy experiences.

But those are other stories.

ON THE ROAD, JACK

Although injuries caused me to stop playing back in 1972, I continued to be involved in rugby in a series of roles such as a referee and a coach for about eight years. I then spent over twenty years travelling and then working abroad. When I retired, at the turn of the century and came back to live in the UK, I bought a house close to my sons' school in Hampshire. Via watching my sons playing the game, both at school and thereafter, I enjoyed the renewal of my association with the grass roots of Rugby Union.

Whilst much, superficially, had changed, this was natural. Nothing in life stands still; it evolves or dies. Underneath, however, the essence and ethos of the game had remained very much the same, I was delighted to discover. One aspect that had evolved more than most, however, was the manner in which players travelled to away matches, and most particularly the first teams of the smaller rugby clubs.

When I played, coaches were seldom employed to carry teams to away matches. This was essentially a cost constraint; most small clubs were battling to buy and/or renovate their clubhouses and the use of a hired coach was regarded as an unnecessary luxury. Remember, too, that this was in the days before leagues were introduced and most clubs therefore arranged block fixtures through the local or the London Fixtures Exchange. Thus, if a club ran five sides, as was pretty much the norm, each week they'd be sending either two or three sides away and that meant, inclusive of non-playing selectors, girlfriends and the odd supporters (and they were indeed odd, believe me), the need would not be for a mini-bus, even if they'd existed then, but a full-blown, 45–52 seater coach. This would be quite an expensive undertaking and there would always be the chance, probably 50/50, that the match between the bottom-most teams would be cancelled and that, typically, would often occur at about midday on the Saturday via receipt of an embarrassed telephone call, just as you were about to set off.

It would also be true to say that, back then, coach firms willing to let rugby clubs hire their vehicles were rare indeed and those that did so were quite often on the verge of bankruptcy, certainly afterwards if not before. One reason for such reluctance to hire out their vehicles would be that the journeys back could prove fairly horrendous, albeit mostly for the drivers and, subsequently, for the cleaners. Looking back, it's no wonder; the mental processes of the passengers had usually been significantly impaired by not ungenerous amounts of beer, and that doesn't allow for those who were of dubious intelligence without any alcoholic depressants. In consequence, the treasurers of most small clubs would only be prepared to accede to the pleadings of the team captains concerned to hire a coach if the venue was a considerable distance hence, and where they'd also been assured there was a definite shortage of players' cars available to make the journey.

From my experiences, this century, of travelling on a team bus when supporting my two sons on their away matches, the journeys back, thankfully, have been comparatively pleasant and lacking in fear for personal embarrassment or safety. Additionally, such singing as occurred was the rendering of pop songs from the 1960s and 1970s, although you had to be pretty knowledgeable to recognise them, so generally incapable of singing in tune were those involved. I think it would be fair to say that the ability to bellow in any key, however inappropriate, was evidently considered a far more valuable contribution to the choral ensemble. By contrast, as I recall coach trips made when I had been a player, there was always at least one individual who would finish up stripped naked whilst the girlfriends on the coach made wholly unconvincing attempts not to watch. If he was lucky, the lad concerned might be given his pants back just before we arrived at our own clubhouse; if unlucky, he might be shovelled out into the cold night without a stitch at least five miles from home. Once, for reasons that I never understood then (and certainly don't now), a potential internecine war between the grunts (forwards) and the big girls' blouses (backs) was temporarily halted when both sides armed themselves with raw eggs brought from John, a student on board returning home with his groceries. Initially, it all started innocently enough with the first two eggs changing hands for about one shilling each, or 5p in today's money. At the time, a shilling was without doubt extortionate since I doubt that John had paid that amount for the entire dozen he'd bought. But the price of one shilling an egg was soon exceeded significantly as other would-be powers on the bus realised that, without their own independent nuclear deterrent, things could go very wrong for them.

All twelve eggs having changed hands (with John imposing a strict condition of sale that he was not to become a subsequent target under any circumstances), an uneasy truce was declared. Not wholly surprisingly, it did not last long. One or two of the more bellicose, armed, would-be combatants began casually throwing their eggs up and down in the air, like Chicago hoods were portrayed in films tossing coins, but all the while keeping careful watch upon those who they suspected would be the most likely aggressors. Doomsday, when it occurred, came from a slightly unexpected cause. Chris, our first fifteen scrumhalf, a cocky, obnoxious, little sod at the best of times (aren't all scrumhalves?), had been lobbing his egg up and down with what he clearly imagined was increasing menace when disaster occurred; he threw the egg a little too high and, when it dropped back into his hand, it cracked and broke.

His expression instantly changing from smug self-confidence to pained disbelief, he stared at the mixed yolk and white of his egg seeping out of the broken shell, through his fingers and onto his trouser legs. In retrospect, the ensuing look of horrified dismay that next passed over his face was less to do with the gooey mess now dribbling down each leg than with the realisation of the Armageddon that was about to materialise. And so it did, O my best beloved, in spades, as all the other possessors of eggs, immediately recognising the changed balance of power, launched their weapons.

Eggs rained in upon Chris from all sides, not just from those he probably regarded as his most likely opponents but also from those he'd probably have regarded as his allies and supporters. Indeed, it was noticeable that the most devastating damage was caused by his flyhalf. That worthy launched his egg with grievous force, a look of pure demonical glee on his face. Mind you, he had received even more looped, hospital passes than usual that afternoon from Chris.

For Chris, the rest of the journey back home, even after he'd extracted a soggy, mud-stained towel from his kit with which he'd done his best to remove the worst of detritus from the ruins of his clothing, was clearly not the most enjoyable. For the rest of us, warm and content, it was a splendidly pleasurable experience, regularly reinforced with glances at Chris' glum expression. Just as well no one lit a match near him; crispy duck would not have been in it.

As a general rule, though, a lot of coach journeys were very much of a muchness with the result that their memories tend to run into one another, such that it's difficult to separate them out. Firstly, they certainly nearly always involved a steady deterioration of relations between the passengers and the driver, most of which was undeniably the fault of the passengers. This regrettable state of affairs would quite often start when, instead of being ready to leave for home at the appointed hour, the driver would be sitting in an empty coach in increasing frustration as the Saturday night's entertainment he'd planned when he got back started going down the tubes. Entering into the adjacent clubhouse, no matter how diplomatically he'd explain the need to leave as soon as possible to those of the rugby club nominally in charge, he'd typically be met with a wide variety of procrastination. Mostly affable if wholly without sense, they'd range from unbelieving dismissals of it being that time already too friendly invitations not to worry but to sit down and have a drink. If the driver was an old hand at this and was not that much surprised, he'd try and retain a smile on his face (even though it would better be described as gritted teeth) and, gathering what support he could from the older members of his coach party, he'd gradually usher them all back and onto the coach.

Except it would never be all. There'd always be one or two who'd somehow escaped the rounding-up process, usually to have a piss. Or there'd be someone who'd left his kit in the changing room and, suddenly remembering it, was blundering around in the dark trying to find it. Worst of all were the amorous playboys who'd chatted up one of the local bicycles. On one such occasion, as it was gleefully relayed to the rest of us back on the coach, Bobby had cajoled a local female to come with him round the back of the clubhouse where, I'm told, he was having a knee-trembler. Whatever that was. Perhaps a condition caused by the excitement of such an unexpected return of his platonic friendliness?

Then, when the headcount was correct, off we'd go; first stop, home. Except there would always be demands for other stops, some imperious, others forlorn and plaintive, and it would never be an incident free journey back. There would always be those who were keen to extend the evening and, under the guise of desperately needing a piss, would clamour for the driver to stop at the next pub. Of course, once they were off the coach, far from wending their way to the outside urinal, they'd make a concerted move to the bar. And so rounding up all the miscreants would start all over again, with any patience the driver had left being inexorably shredded to pieces. If we had an experienced driver, he'd know exactly what Machiavellian schemes were being planned and, rather than pulling into a pub's car park, he'd pull up in a dark, muddy, unlit lay-by. Most of the men on board would then troop off the coach and, standing side-by-side in the black of the night, legs apart and backs to the coach, would empty their straining bladders through billowing clouds of steam into a ditch or whatever. Sometimes, those who'd been sitting at the back of the bus (which generally marked them down as the most likely to be anti-social in all things) could not get off the coach fast enough. On such occasions, and where they couldn't readily get past those either still urinating or who'd already finished and who were attempting to clamber back inside, those last off the coach, almost doubled up with the effort of containing themselves, would take the easy way out and simply relieve their internal pressures by pissing on the backs of the legs of those lined up in front of them. Whilst this behaviour was often regarded with great hilarity by those who had performed it, it was seldom regarded as humorous by those on the receiving end, and their debates over this behaviour could become both heated and protracted, prompting further delay.

But if these coach journeys are now difficult to recall individually, another journey remains indelibly etched in my mind when, many years ago, I guested for an extremely hospitable but somewhat impecunious rugby club in the Wirral. For some seasons, they had experienced considerable problems in transporting teams to away matches. Then, in a magnificently innovative gesture, one of their older members, who owned a furniture removal company, donated to them one of his older vans. This, although slow and mechanically less than wholly reliable, was enormous and was not only capable, at a squeeze, of accommodating up to three away teams but also a number of happy and raucous supporters, plus a few blazers. These away trips became an adventure in themselves, since the more imaginative and less inhibited of their members kitted out the interior with old settees and armchairs rescued from the local dump. Actually, I'm not sure they were too selective in their choice of such items since they brought with them a distinctly offensive odour and I was told, in hushed confidential whispers on more than one occasion, that the rats that'd made their nests inside had happily acceded to the upgrade in neighbourhood.

Come to think of it, the inside of that van was more than just mildly malodorous; on first entry it distinctly jerked you upright. For that and other medical reasons, the club's fathers also had a travelling bar installed, consisting of about twenty crates of beer and about half a dozen bottles each of gin and whisky; certainly you needed something strong when you first boarded this vehicle.

But I digress. On returning home from a successful away match in the Vale of Lune one Saturday night, we suddenly realised our jollifications were in danger of being disturbed when we distinctly felt our mobile clubhouse slowing down. At first, not much thought was given to this; either the driver or his mate probably wanted a piss; it certainly wouldn't be us. Then, as we came to a gentle halt, above the mixed din of one group of singers and the others engaged in conversation, we realised we could hear a police siren very close to the rear of the van. Cautiously moving up the big roller-blind that came down from the roof of the vehicle at its rear, the inside of the van became illuminated more and more strongly with a flashing blue light and we could then see a police car had stopped about 12-15 yards behind us. Both its doors were open and the two police officers who'd been inside were chatting with our driver and his mate whilst gesturing to a trail of fluid that, illuminated by the police car's headlights, started from beneath our van and ran on under the police car before disappearing into the dark beyond.

Since none of us in the van had the slightest idea of what was going on (and saw no reason to be enlightened, especially after the rugby club's secretary, a lawyer of apparently considerable renown in the local magistrate's court, hoarsely advised us all to say now't and keep stumm), we all stood there, swaying blissfully in the stationery vehicle. After a short discussion, presumably covering their who are you, where are you going and where have you come from information needs, one of the police officers plus our driver crouched down to more closely examine this trail of fluid, now noticeably less than before. "Doesn't smell like petrol," observed the police officer.

"Certainly isn't oil," said his partner, chipping in his two penny worth. "Not viscous enough."

The first officer then looked at the driver and asked, "Have you been having any trouble with your radiator of late, sir?" Before receiving an answer he looked back at the van and continued, "Your vehicle is a little on the aged side, after all."

The second policeman also turned to view our van and realised that they had an unexpected audience watching them in a happy silence. Fortunately, this was before the days of not uncommon smuggling of immigrants into the country so he simply stared at us in surprise before asking of our driver's mate, "Who are they?"

Both an immediate answer having been supplied plus, for whatever reason, the history of the ownership of the van, the second policeman snorted and turned back to the problem at hand. Returning to his original question, he commented, "Doesn't look like water, Harry. Not only that but it has some aroma, although I can't immediately place it."

The first officer nodded in agreement then dipped a forefinger in the fluid and cautiously sniffed it. "It's definitely not petrol," he confirmed, shaking his head. He sniffed his finger again, perplexed. "I know the smell but just can't identify it." He then licked his forefinger gently with his tongue and shook his head yet again.

"Here, Harry," said his partner, "Let me have a sniff." He did so, looked non-plussed for a moment and then a look of surprised recognition passed across his face. "That's not petrol, or water – it's urine!"

At this identification of the fluid, it was as if a great illuminating light had been turned on for us listening in the back of the van and we almost all turned, as one, to stare at the source of what we realised would almost certainly turn out to be the origin of this incident. Those remarkable and far-sighted fathers of the club, recognising that, for distant away matches when not only carrying a substantial number of determined and professional alcohol imbibers but also catering for their avid and semi-inexhaustible thirsts, it would be practical to plan for their ongoing needs to satisfy the requirements of nature. As a result, another element of their conversion of the furniture van for the club members' comfort had been to cut a hole about a foot across in one corner of the van's floor. In consequence, there was never any need, when travelling to and from away games for journeys to be interrupted by anxious demands to stop for a while. You simply moved to the hole in the corner of the van and, with a glorious feeling of relief, let it all go.

The first police officer, having spent more than a few seconds spitting on the floor and wiping his mouth with his handkerchief with some vigour, wanted to book everyone in sight but couldn't think of any law we'd transgressed. The second officer, by comparison, vainly trying to keep a straight face, was much more interested in getting back to the station to spread the news of this traffic incident, no doubt suitably and extravagantly embellished.

Sadly, I later heard that, when details of this event reached the ears of more senior members of the local constabulary, a less relaxed and appreciative view was taken and, following a short inspection of the van it was declared un-roadworthy.

Or were the authorities taking the piss?

MIDNIGHT CRUISE

As varied and educational as have been my other travelling experiences within the UK, it is difficult to remember anything that could really claim to match up to the time in my first rugby club that was forever known as "The Night We Stole the Gravesend Ferry".

It had been such a comparatively peaceful and law-abiding night up until then, too. Our first and third teams had both played away in Kent against Gravesend. Old opponents and beloved foes that they were, we had expected hard-fought games in which any number of devious, underhand tricks and despicable, wholly unfair techniques would be employed. In consequence, we'd almost certainly have to inflict dubious retaliations before they'd committed an originating first offense. Judging by the passionate exhortations that emanated from their changing rooms before the match, they would be similarly entering into the true spirit of the game. None of us were disappointed and, having sluiced off the mud (and, in the case of the Extra A, the slimier portions of cow pats from their playing fields reportedly nearer Dover than Gravesend), we settled down to an evening's entertainment devised by the mentally challenged for the mentally retarded. That most of these wholly pointless and mostly inexplicable antics were performed by individuals who would often go on to become successful doctors, dentists, lawyers, accountants and schoolmasters probably provides a worrying assessment of our society. It's true that not everyone present behaved in such fashion; regrettably there were also some truly verbose and embarrassing louts amongst us, but they were mostly destined to become the sad failures in our society, such as politicians or estate agents.

On this particular evening, things had actually gone really swimmingly. So much so in fact, that we'd overlooked the passage of time. Ordinarily, that would have been of little significance; we'd have all tumbled out of our host's clubhouse when the time felt right, have got into our cars and toddled off home. However, when playing at Gravesend there was, before the day of the Dartford Tunnel, not only an additional hurdle to overcome in the shape of the River Thames, but we had been warned in advance by our hosts that the Kent Police was having a blitz on drinking and driving. Happily, there existed a reasonable alternative – public transport.

A material percentage of our players worked in London and travelled there by train each day via the Fenchurch Street line. For this purpose, they all had season tickets and, by some quirk of the regulations beyond our understanding, these season tickets not only enabled the holders to travel from Southend or other stations direct to London, but also via the loop-line which went down to Tilbury. If you then disembarked from the train at Tilbury, it was less than a mile's walk to the ferry for Gravesend, and from its terminal on the other side of the river it was but a short walk up the hill to catch a bus that went past the grounds of Gravesend RFC.

As useful and convenient as this was, all these modes of public transport worked to reasonably strict schedules. Even so, when we finally bid our adieus to our hosts and straggled over to the bus stop, no-one realised that events had already been set in play for the unlikely chaos that would ensue. Once the bus had arrived and the hardened merrymakers that had stayed to the bitter end had boarded it and swamped the upper deck, one or two of the less intellectually challenged began to voice thoughts as to the time of the last ferry. Their nascent concerns were quickly assuaged by the loudly proclaimed assurances of the know-it-all not to worry as the ferries ran all night; well, at least up to midnight. Didn't they?

By the time we'd reached Gravesend and clambered off the bus in West Street, it had just gone, from memory, about 10 pm. From West Street, it was but a short walk down the hill to the ferry terminal and those amongst us of nervous dispositions had had their concerns reasonably allayed by the sight of a ferry just arriving to dock from Tilbury. Even so, they had to be almost forcibly persuaded to join the rest of us in shouldering our way into a fish and chip shop on the way down the hill. Thereafter, trying to balance the need to carry our kit bags whilst holding bags of crisply battered fish, greasy chips and large pickled onions all contained within editions of last week's newspapers, we sauntered down to the waiting ferry.

And that's where our troubles began.

Back then, in the very early 1960s, a dual service ran between Gravesend and Tilbury; there were separate ferries for vehicles and also for passengers travelling on foot. The vehicles ferries were the larger vessels and pretty ugly, too. Essentially, they were large and open-decked, with a small, central control section from which the captain and his mercantile officers controlled the vessels, each probably of about 450-500 tons displacement. If you caught this ferry you had the choice of remaining in your car for the journey or getting out and climbing about three flights of stairs to stand on top of the control section, just behind the flying bridge. All this was out in the open and, since it had just started to rain, we were all thankful it was not one of these car ferries we were catching but one that solely catered for foot passengers.

Except that we weren't. Because, when we arrived at the vessel awaiting us, this was a car ferry and, when we asked when the next passenger ferry would be leaving for Tilbury, the short answer was tomorrow; we'd missed the last one that night, and by a considerable margin.

This, whilst considered a bloody nuisance, was not immediately viewed as a catastrophe as the obvious and thankfully instantly available alternative was the rather beaten-up vessel in front of us. Having circumnavigated what to us was the clearly pedantic and obnoxious official who claimed that our return tickets were invalid for the car ferry by simply walking around him en masse, we were shepherded up the stairs to the top of the control section by the few deck-hands braving the elements. Given the increasing volume and speed of the rain being driven across this metal eerie, we clustered together in increasing misery in the lee of the vessel's funnel. By this time, recriminations had started to set in, and hard questions were being asked as to what mindless sod had claimed the passenger ferries ran all night. I took no part in all this; I was still a teenager and regarded as a young apprentice by my elders and betters. In any event, I felt it would be much more in my interests to keep well out of any inquisition that might be about to take place.

As often happens in situations like this, once the happy unthinking camaraderie that had previously enveloped and carried us down to the ferry had been pierced, more cogent reasoning was applied to our plight. And the potential facts that began to emerge from our earlier cocoon of well-being were not promising. "Just a minute," said one slightly worried voice, "doesn't the last passenger ferry link up with the last train back to Southend?"

A moment's silence followed whilst this possibility was digested. "Shit!" was the communal response, both spoken and thought, and then another, more optimistic soul added, "Maybe; but I'm fairly sure that there's still another train that would take us to Fenchurch Street, from where we could catch a train back home."

"Are you out of your mind?" asked another bedraggled figure. "It's after 10.30 pm now and, by the time we've got off this ship and then run all the way to Tilbury Station it'll be after 11 pm. So, even if there is another train to London and it leaves straight away, we won't get to Fenchurch Street until nearly midnight."

"And the only trains home after midnight," put in a knowingly lugubrious voice, "are all-station stoppers."

"All right then, clever dick," retorted the earlier, positively-minded speaker caustically to his detractors, "what alternatives do we have?"

The dismal silence lasted more than a few minutes whilst we all contemplated this less than happy ending to our day, particularly those married individuals who'd given cavalier assurances to their wives that of course they wouldn't be back too late; sure, they promised. Now, the thought of being rounded up by the Gestapo was beginning to look a far preferable option. Shortly afterwards, these gloomy musings were blasted asunder as an ear-blasting boom from the ship's horn just a few feet above us and to our right not only frightened the shit out of us but signalled the ferry's slow move away from the dock and out into the river.

Once most of us had regained our shattered senses, we found that the change in direction by the ferry meant we no longer had much shelter from the rain. We shuffled forwards but, keeping in the lee of the funnel, were now placed right behind the flying bridge. As we arrived there, suddenly, right under our noses, from out of a trapdoor in the floor of the flying bridge, up popped a young deck officer. All of us were taken a little aback at this unexpected meeting but the young deck officer made much more of it than we did. Having gestured to us emphatically to move away from the railings that separated us from him and then waited imperiously until we'd done so, he took to walking backwards and forwards along the flying bridge.

This flying bridge was probably less than two yards wide and ran from one side of the ferry to the other. Along its length were stanchions at about head height and about four or five yards apart and, passing through a hole at the top of each stanchion, was a thickish wire that, at both ends of the flying bridge then ran up to the horn on the funnel that had so nearly caused a mass release from our bowels. Unfortunately, although most of us had calmed these internal organs somewhat, two of our number, and the least controllable and most mischievous ones at that, had not only recovered from that shock but were contemplating a fresh bout of lunatic activities of which the rest of us had yet to become aware.

And that's when our troubles really started.

After a brief, muttered, conversation between the two of them whilst the rest of us gazed on in dulled disinterest, Brian and Freddie gently moved, separately, to each end of the flying bridge. Then, when the young deck officer reached the end of it and was standing close to the innocent-looking Freddie, Brian reached up and yanked on the wire to the ship's horn just above him. The ensuing blast not only threatened to induce further physical and mental sufferings amongst everyone else but wholly convulsed the young deck officer. Spinning like a demented top, his mouth wide agape, he bellowed something unintelligible at Brian and hurtled along the flying bridge towards that miscreant. But just as he was about to remonstrate with Brian, Freddie reached up at the other end of the flying bridge and repeated the trick. Caught almost in mid-air, and before he could deal with Brian, the young deck officer made a wondrously acrobatic turn and raced back towards Freddie.

Well, you can guess what happened next, can't you? All in all, I think Brian and Freddie blew that bloody horn six or seven times before the sailor boy's nerved cracked. Apprehending he was not only grossly out-numbered but also tactically out-manoeuvred, he lifted the trapdoor on the flying bridge and shot down the steps below to fetch the cavalry. By this time, some of the other, more devil-may-care and unprincipled members of our group had awoken to what they manifestly considered to be a magnificent jape. Accordingly, three of them climbed over the rails around the flying bridge and stood on its trapdoor, right next to a deck telegraph.

And that's when our troubles really and truly began.

After over fifty years, my memories of exactly what happened next, and why, are more than a little imprecise. Although that isn't wholly due to the amount of alcohol I'd imbibed that night, I'll go as far as to say that it might not have helped. Certainly, my memories were distinctly lacking in any real clarity even the next morning. What I do remember is Graham climbing over the same rails to join the three witches and there being an increasingly loud argument over the next course of action. To add further to this pantomime of complete and utter mayhem, there were also heavy blows being rained on the underside of the trapdoor and a number of instructions being joyfully rung via almost continual use of the deck telegraph to what could only have been an utterly confused engine room. And all this was interspersed by the musical accompaniment provided by Brian and Freddie on the ferry's horn, where they seemed to come together nicely in an unusual jam session.

I also recall that the argument between Graham and the three witches becoming increasingly acrimonious. The subject of their disagreement seemed to be over who should have control of the deck telegraph. It's all more than a little hazy now but, to a land-lubber like me, it was as if they were talking in code. "What d'you mean, you're more qualified to take charge of the telegraph?" Alan, one of the three witches demanded truculently.

"Because I spent the last couple of years of the war in the navy," retorted Graham belligerently.

"Yeah," replied his younger antagonist, "but you were only in the Wavy Navy, not the Andrew!"

Wavy Navy? Andrew? What the hell were they talking about? It was only some time later that it was explained to me that "Andrew" had originally been a slang name for any man onward in the Royal Navy. Allegedly harking back to the 1800s when an Andrew Miller was a supplier of provisions to the Royal Navy, he had such an apparent monopoly that he was said to own both the Navy and its ships. And Wavy Navy? Up until 1952, officers in the Royal Naval Reserve had wavy sleeve rings to differentiate them from the full-time professionals in the Royal Navy, whose sleeve rings were straight. Whilst officers in the RNR proved themselves, over a considerable period of time, to be as equally proficient as their peers in the Royal Navy, the latter liked to decry and denigrate those from the RNR.

"Maybe," came Graham's caustic reply, "but how much service did you see in World War 2 – only thing you fought for were sweet rations!"

This accusation clearly ratcheted up the tension between the two individuals, both of them with their hands wrapped around the handle of the deck telegraph whilst the ferry idled its way down river. The response, when it came after a few seconds of glaring antagonism between the parties was a deft blow from Alan. "In any event, what would you know about navigation; you were only a fucking stoker!"

Rather stunned by this reminder, Graham fell back on a weak rejoinder. "All right, but at least I was in the navy."

His opponent moved in for the kill. "Doing what? Shoveling coal? They can train fucking monkeys to do that! I'll bet you never even came up on deck when you were at sea!"

"Yes, I did!" returned Graham, albeit without any really discernible conviction.

"Yeah, right," replied Alan, "probably to have a fag or a piss over the side."

How long did this disgraceful nonsense last? I really don't have a clue. How far down the river did we manage to take the ferry? Again, I have no real idea. Some claim we got as far down the Thames as the Ford works at Dagenham but I don't recall any of those making such claim being present. Fact is, over the intervening years, if all those who've claimed they took part were actually there we'd have needed the Ark Royal to have been requisitioned for ferry duties that night.

What I do remember, albeit through a foggy haze, was a loud warning from Brian at his end of the flying bridge. "Look out," he shouted, "Rozzers! We're about to be boarded!"

Indeed, the ferry was boarded by a number of officers from a police launch. No attempt was actually made to stop them, although Brian had to be restrained from hurling life belts at them as they crossed from the launch to the ferry.

In the end, the ferry successfully made the crossing to Tilbury and we were all marched nearly a mile up the road to Tilbury Police Station. I'm sure that most of us would probably have settled for a night in a warm cell there with some relief, but it had been a busy night in the town and there was no room at the inn. Instead, and to the scarcely hidden amusement of the police, we were marched across the road to Tilbury Railway Station, where we were given a severe blocking by an increasingly sarcastic and irate senior police officer, thus probably deliberately preventing us from catching the last train from Tilbury to London. After that, and ignoring the suggestions of the lunatics amongst us who wanted to walk home the 18-20 miles along the railway lines, we dossed down, wet and miserable, on the platforms.

Looking at this experience dispassionately, I have to say that, if this had happened today, we'd have all appeared in court, been fined considerable amounts and probably locked up. And quite right, too. As I stated earlier, life continually evolves, but not always wholly for the better. We had acted in a phenomenally stupid way but the police, less constrained than at present by PC, handled it all with great intelligence and even greater tolerance.

Mind you, I would still have preferred to spend the night in the nick, with a decent cup of tea next morning before I was pushed out. Christ, it was bloody cold and uncomfortable trying to sleep on that railway platform, out in the open. Since that time, despite what you see in the advertisements on the TV, I've never really fancied a cruise.

CHARGE OF THE HEAVY BRIGADE

Although rugby tours to just about anywhere are experiences to be savoured (and those I went on become ever more memorable as time passes by and senility catches up), for me, those made to France were always the most anticipated and, to the best of my now admittedly somewhat hazy memories, those that best fulfilled their truly extravagant expectations. It didn't really matter to where you went in France, the extraordinarily and almost excessive hospitality and joie de vivre with which you'd be met never wavered. Probably, those I went on to south-west France were the most remarkable in this respect as, often with games played against or held in small towns and even villages, the overwhelming impression you'd receive was that every single local citizen was not only aware of the match shortly to be played against the visiting "Rostbifs" but was also passionately involved in ensuring that the celebrations laid on for them would be as exhausting off the field as on it.

Even so, probably the majority of rugby tours were made to Paris, principally (as it was claimed to not unreasonably suspicious wives, fiancées and girlfriends) so as to watch France play against England on the Saturday. Certainly, over the years, I have made well over ten such visits there. Unfortunately, I also have to confess that my recollections of tours to that wonderful city nearly always include what, in retrospect, were disgracefully childish behaviour by gangs of British males of all ages let off the leash there. Watching the international itself was generally not the problem; it was the evening's riotous celebrations in the city of light that followed, win or lose, that were so excessive. Furthermore, these antics on the Saturday night rendered the game organised for the touring party on the Sunday against a local team of usually wholly unknown quality what became a truly awful if not frightening experience. Guest players from such as the Royal Marines would confide afterwards it was the most horrific 80 minutes of their lives, with players crawling off the field to regurgitate the previous night's food and drink with such vehemence that all or any of the resulting sounds, sights and aromas would induce others, desperately trying to ignore the churning contents of their stomach, to follow suit.

Not only that but, although a few of us had experienced the level of ferocity with which games between two local rugby clubs were played in France, many English players naively went into these games believing they would be played in a spirit of great bonhomie; a true, physical reflection of the concorde and courtesy with which they'd been met when they arrived at their hosts' grounds.

Wrong. Whatever was said off the field and no matter how many times cheeks were kissed in apparently fond if embarrassing greeting, once they got you onto the pitch, just about every French player did his very best to beat the crap out of you, by fair means or foul. To be fair to the French players, this level of apparently wholly gratuitous violence was not something that had been especially reserved and practised for the game against the visiting rostbifs however you might be convinced otherwise; this was their standard level of behaviour for any domestic game, as I discovered when guesting on a number of occasions for a French side captained by a friend of mine. Then, much to my initial wide-eyed amazement and fury, nothing seemed to be off-limit. Punches to the head and body, kicks anywhere, even bites of any fleshy part of the body seemed to be de rigueur if not mandatory. And God help you if you were trapped on the bottom of a rock with your head sticking outside it. Furthermore, in those early days our boots were not the soft, almost slip-on types they are now; they were fitted with steel toe-caps. And as daunting a thought as that might be, what was even more intimidating and definitely at least as painful were the leather studs that were nailed to your boots. The nastiest aspect of these was that although the leather studs would get worn down over less than a season, the metal nails would not. Thus players would not infrequently end games with cuts and scratches over just about any part of their bodies such that they looked as if they'd been ten rounds with a Bengal tiger.

Such, then, were the kinds of greeting you could expect to receive from the opposing team when you played against the frogs, wherever that might be. Indeed, there was one French player with whom, over a period of some 12 years, I had a running battle every time I played against him. It all began when I was just seventeen, picked for the first time for my club's 1st XV against a visiting team of frogs. We kicked off, the ball went straight into touch for the first line-out and, having lined up for the throw-in, the next thing I knew I was flat on my back with my nose pumping blood. And there, beaming down at me, was my opposite number, Claude.

Although, off the field, we not only became very good friends but remained so until his death a couple of years ago, this was the kind of attention I came to expect from him every time we played against each other. Of course, once beaten, twice shy, and I only needed those lessons that seemed to come my way almost continually during that first game. During the first half, I wandered around, somewhat dazedly, wondering what the bloody hell I'd done to upset Claude but then, at half time, I was forcibly instructed by my older, more gnarled team-mates to return Claude's compliments and knock the shit out of him. Thus, seemingly having been given carte blanche by my own side, but taking care to ensure the referee was always elsewhere, I set to with a will. When the final whistle blew, Claude immediately looked around him and, spotting me about thirty yards away, jerked his head up and shambled purposefully (if that's not an oxymoron) towards me. Looking at his face, which now boasted a closed left eye and a missing front tooth, I thought, shit, this mad fucking frog wants to continue this battle even though the game's over. But, again to my amazement, Claude grabbed my right hand with his own and embraced me with his left arm, all the while mumbling "Un grand jeu, mon ami, trés formidable," through his swollen lips

This I learned, was the reason why Claude played rugby. An ex-paratrooper, he had never played rugby before joining the French forces and, being more than a little lacking in both the skills and the concepts of the game, seemed convinced that it had been devised to enable him to legally and joyfully engage in authorised mayhem. Claude had then been over thirty-five, but he only retired when nearing fifty. Since his behaviour on the pitch never varied and I became bigger, stronger and more devious over the next twelve or so years whilst his powers waned, the succeeding years' battles became more and more tilted in my favour. Nevertheless, his appetite for the fray remained undiminished, as did his enthusiasm for energetic post-match revelries.

Indeed, on looking back at our visits to France, more energy and skill was probably spent during these revelries on ridiculous pranks and drinking games in the more salacious parts of Paris during Saturday night and Sunday morning than was ever evident in the Sunday afternoon game that followed. Such events were varied in the extreme but that which still kindles memories, even 50 years later, is the game of "belly charging". At that time, in the UK, this was usually played in clubhouses reasonably early in the evening, provided that sufficient alcohol had been drunk to give the participants a wholly irrational and unjustified belief in their superiority over their opponents. Additionally, from their team-mates (mostly from those not participating) they were encouraged into a sense of misplaced optimism in their likelihood of success. Lastly, this game was usually played before the combatants became both physically and mentally incapable, although the latter element of this statement is arguable.

The attraction of this "game" was that, for the participants, it was extremely easy to grasp and, for the spectators, immensely amusing in that at least one (and possibly both) of the competitors in each match was highly likely to make himself an even bigger fool than he'd been created. Essentially, two competitors would face each other, about ten or more yards apart, hands locked behind their backs. Then, when the appointed referee said, "Go", they would charge towards each other and, just before colliding, would put their shoulders back and push their bellies out. This resulted in a physical impact of quite considerable proportions since, with both competitors reaching the dizzying speed of about ten miles per hour, it was like throwing oneself off a twelve foot high brick wall, belly down, to land on the pavement below at double that speed.

Even for the more experienced and knowledgeable competitor, the consequences could be disastrous. Not only could one's self confidence be deflated or drained, but so could one's stomach, and not just if one had apparently come off worse in the actual collision.

There were also distinct ethics to be followed. It was absolutely critical that, at the point of impact, each competitor thrust his belly forward; not to do so, and to lead with either the chest or, worse, a dropped shoulder, was an unforgivable sin in the same league as kissing your sister or raping the Queen. Indeed, if the assembled crowd considered a competitor had thus infringed on the ethos of the sport, copious volumes of beer would be hurled over such individual. Quite right, too.

However, whilst the British have generally been the fathers and ambassadors of the majority of sports that are now played across the world, this one has never seemed to catch on elsewhere, although valiant efforts have been made to educate such as the French in its nuances and subtleties, especially during the weekends when England was playing France in Paris, mostly back in the days when this occurred at Stade de Colombes. Sadly, probably due to a lack of understanding as to the comparative effects of having drunk more than two of three pints of red wine as compared to IPA, the venue chosen was not ideal. Whilst a carriage on the Metro was the perfect length, the manner in which it swayed vigorously between stations caused a number of the competitors charging up (or down) the aisle of the carriage to plunge to one side, thus generally flattening some amazed and petrified Parisians seated thereabouts. For reasons difficult to comprehend, the Parisians seemed unable to grasp the exquisite humour of such situations, and were even less amused with the projectile vomiting that sometimes occurred when the combatants met. Ah well, we all know the French are a strange and emotionally immature lot.

In this respect, the bout that most sticks in my memory could have been categorised as a domestic one, even though it occurred on an only half-full Metro train in Paris. Whilst our club's representative team was supposed to consist of a full 1st XV, full of experienced, hardened quasi-athletes, it was far from that. As usual, many of the younger, more competent but sadly more impecunious players (especially those at university) were unable to participate. This meant that, faced with a touring party containing almost twice as many alickadoos as players, the doors had to be opened to other players, including not only guests claimed to be highly skilled representatives of other clubs (usually total fabrications) but also members who generally played for our lower teams. One such individual was Graham, the aging bachelor who usually turned out for our 4th XV.

Now, those who have played at Colombes or watched international rugby there will know that it was (and maybe still is) one of the least hospitable locations in France. Then, not only were there no bars nor other facilities serving liquid refreshments inside the ground, but it also only boasted about two cafés in the streets around. These cafés, which had never even been considered for recommendation by Michelin, even for their tyres, could host at most, including standing outside and blocking up the road for 50 metres in each direction, about four hundred customers each. By comparison, the crowd that exited from Stade de Colombes eager for refreshment and entertainment numbered about thirty thousand. In consequence, those in the know (and the alickadoos were always in the know about such things) had taken care to make detailed plans to combat such a truly terrible, restrictive and soul-destroying situation. We had all thus enjoyed a suitably copious liquid brunch and, less anyone began to suffer withdrawal symptoms before we could get back to central Paris, a large and impressive collection of hip flasks had been filled with selections of whisky, rum, Cognac and Armagnac. This brilliant strategic planning had proved remarkably perceptive, since it proved necessary to make full use of these medicinal stores; I don't remember quite why but I can assure you that it did prove so. We were thus travelling back into Paris from Colombes when we came to realise that, at the other end of that Metro carriage was a similar touring group hailing from an East London club whom we had played against on many a memorable, bloody but friendly occasion. Contact between the two groups having been cordially re-established by the long-standing and peculiarly English courtesy of shouting insults at one another, it was somehow agreed that an excellent way to get the evening off to a flying start would be to hold a belly-charging contest. I couldn't be sure, even at the time, but I feel fairly confident that Graham was one of the moving lights in this arrangement, especially as he had long prided himself on being not only a seasoned but an expert exponent of this highly skilled activity.

After agreeing the variations to be accepted to the standard rules, most of which involved how to resolve any unfair intervention by the French passengers who, rather ungraciously and completely without any real justification, refused to give up their seats or leave a completely clear passage for the combatants to hurl themselves down the carriage towards each other. This disdainful refusal by the French passengers to join in what would obviously be good, clean English fun was most disappointing; the French talk very superciliously about their culture but seem to have little interest in or tolerance for that of others.

Having agreed the ground rules, most of our opposition from East London then seemed initially not too enthusiastic to begin the tournament, no-one wishing to volunteer to be their first-up representative. However, virtually unknown to most of his colleagues, their captain, a devious bastard if ever there was one, had a real ace up his sleeve, the realisation they had a new recruit who might well be absolutely ideal. This was a lad in his early twenties who, we learned subsequently, had yet to play his first game of rugby and had only been persuaded to come on their tour to Paris by a cousin appointed to recruit bodies to fill empty seats on the charter flight. He was simply enormous, being approximately 6'7" and weighing about 24 stone; he only needed a bolt in his neck to be a dead ringer for Dr. Frankenstein's monster.

The rules were quickly explained to him by his captain and he nodded happily at the prospect facing him as he was led to the driver's end of the Metro carriage. Graham duly took up his own station by the guard's end but, sizing the two of them up, I began to wonder if Graham had not bitten off rather more than he could chew. Graham, however, was a cunning old sod and had learnt all the dark and devious tricks of the game so, when they both started their charges, there was immense interest in seeing how Graham would deal with this considerable challenge to his reputation and authority.

In the event, it was man against boy. Both competitors rumbled forward joyfully at their top speeds (though Graham's smile was looking increasingly fixed) and, at the last minute, the monster almost skidded to a halt whilst, simultaneously, throwing forward his immense belly with concussive force. Graham rebounded backwards even faster than he came into the impact, his mouth agape, gasping for breath, whilst his legs tried desperately to keep him upright. Fortunately, the French passengers who'd craned forward to watch this clash of the Titans quickly realised that they might be in danger of serious collateral damage from Graham's reverse charge and, with alarmed shouts of warning and adroit sidesteps of which a matador would have been eminently proud, they avoided a secondary major collision. Graham crashed into the door at the rear of the coach and, mouth still attempting desperately to suck air into his deflated lungs and with eyes opened wide in shock, he slowly slid down until he was seated on the floor of the carriage, staring back at his triumphantly beaming opponent.

This fantastic explosion of energy, and Graham's forced retreat at perhaps even greater speed than his advance, was greeted with an astonished silence by our party – nobody could remember the last time our champion had been so explosively and contemptuously trounced. But the coup-de-grace came a few seconds later when a truly shattered Graham, having not only somehow pulled himself together but kept down the contents of his stomach, returned to the centre of the coach, clutching his midriff and looking more than a little green about the gills. His giant opponent lumbered up to him and, clapping him familiarly on the shoulder, enquired, "Best of free?"

In this era of professional rugby, where so many players of wonderful athleticism, fitness and skill are given and no doubt fully follow the carefully calculated diets and exercise routines that are devised for them, I suspect that tours of this nature to Paris or wherever are unlikely to contain such cultural delights.

Shame – they don't know what they're missing.

LE VAINQUEUR

These days, I almost always watch 6 Nations matches between France and England on TV, simply because of the prohibitively high costs of doing so in person. To do so at Twickenham will generally set you back the thick end of £170 per person, being £80 for a ticket, £40 for travelling costs (either by car or by train) and £50 for a meal and refreshments. By comparison, I can watch the match on TV in either my local rugby club, at one of the local pubs or at home for very little; say about £15 at worst, even though I'd much prefer to do so in situ. But, as much as I miss this direct, vicarious involvement, what I would really like to continue to experience are the long weekends in Paris, watching this most wonderful of rivalries and physical confrontations there. For the first few of the many times I've enjoyed a shortened tour of this nature, starting in 1960, the international match was played at Stades Colombes which, to be honest, was a pretty dismal place. It was miles out of the centre of Paris and a goodly walk from the nearest Metro station, with a pitch that was set inside an athletics track. This made it difficult to become greatly involved in the match because not only did it seem to be taking place in the next field but the shallow gradient of the stands (and they were exactly that) meant these placed the action even further away. Furthermore, the players didn't walk on the field from the stands but suddenly appeared from a tunnel that led from their changing rooms to what looked like an allotment hut behind one set of posts. Given the physical state of most of the English supporters, numb with hangovers or still partially inebriated and standing there in benign miscomprehension, in those days the match was often the least remembered part of the weekend.

This all changed vastly for the better when such matches were transferred to Parc des Princes. Indeed, the atmosphere there was superior to just about every other stadium I had visited at that time, in the early 1970s; it was the only one then where there were no individual stands and the nearness of the pitch and the steep raking of the seats meant that the acoustics, at least by the standards of the day, were incredible. This created a wonderful buzz before, during and after the match, no doubt fuelled by the sharing of flasks of whisky and cognac that was required to be performed whenever either side scored. A high scoring match thus resulted in an extremely joyous and amicable crowd. Not only that but it was and remains located on Rue du Commandant Guilbaud, just off the Périphérique, within easy walking distance of Auteuil in the very fashionable and up-market 16th arondissement. This meant that, virtually immediately you left Parc des Princes, you were in areas of Paris positively overflowing with bars and restaurants, wholly unlike the drab environs of Stade de Colombes and the wastelands that surround Stade de France.

For whatever reason (and there are many), a tour to Paris always engendered far more enthusiasm than those arranged within the UK or Ireland. Perhaps for the committed first team members there was a frisson of excitement at measuring their capabilities, both individually and as a team, against the local hard men in Devon or Cornwell, in the West Country or in Wales or Ireland, but to the less committed or skilled players, the games themselves were generally to be avoided if at all possible. What possible pleasure, was the argument, was there in being trapped at the bottom of a ruock and having the shit kicked out of you by a gang of malevolent sadists, many of whom could have passed as orcs without the need for make-up? This always seemed particularly true when playing in Wales or Ireland. In those days, nobody had heard of gumshields and the entire opposition pack probably wouldn't have been able to put together a full set of teeth between them anyway. You thus had to prepare not only for head-butting as the scrum formed, but also having your ears and other protuberances either bitten or given a nasty suck. And it wasn't that much better for those who'd not come along in a playing capacity; whilst the bigger clubs undoubtedly enjoyed far more salubrious surroundings, tours made by smaller clubs always seemed to finish playing on the side of a mountain, particularly in Wales. Not only that but it was mandatory for it to have rained for at least the preceding fortnight, so that not only was the pitch like a paddy field (and I'm not referring solely to Ireland) but the entire surrounding area. Thus the spectators would stand in the pissing rain blown in horizontally by an icy wind whilst a wholly featureless bout of unarmed mud-wrestling took place in front of them. The only thing worse for any such individual would be when, as it seemingly nearly always did, one of the worthies on the field became injured and his team captain would shout across, "Go and get changed, Sid, you're on."

Protests as to not having any kit, of not having played for three or four years, of having some semi-terminal debilitating injury or some foul, virulent and highly contagious disease would be swiftly overcome or ignored. Instead, having been kitted out in an incongruous collection of spare and ill-fitting items, generally still clingingly soggy and muddy, the unfortunate individual concerned would be pushed onto the field, wholly unprepared yet dreading the savagery he was about to encounter that would ruin both his weekend and, quite probably, the following week or so. And players complain these days about the dangers of playing on pitches with a few puddles on them – Christ, I've played on some where we had the alternative option of a water polo contest. Big girls' blouses.

By comparison, even given the known predilection for violence of French players when on the pitch, going on a tour to France, was generally viewed as having won one of the better prizes in life, and particularly if you were a supporter rather than a player. It didn't really matter where exactly you went in France, the hospitality and the charm of the place were invariably magical. Certainly, I always loved visiting clubs in or close to the Pyrenées, at the Atlantic end, the Mediterranean end or simply vaguely in the middle. Even so, it was in Paris that so many of my memories are set in those halcyon days when we would make our bi-annual pilgrimage to that marvellous city. Pilgrimage is probably the wrong word, since the earnestly expressed intent of those travelling was more along the lines of a little rape and pillage. Indeed, these ambitions were nearly always realised; but this was mostly performed by the varied citizens of Paris on their naïve visitors.

Of the very earliest of such tours I regret that I have very little cogent memory and believe that my return to the UK was solely due to my being shepherded by the soft-hearted elder statesman amongst the alickadoos that accompanied the team. I then progressed through the years of my pomp, as a fully-fledged visiting English hooligan, before assuming (not really willingly) the same role of protecting the younger first-trippers, mostly from themselves. In such last role, having preceded the main raiding party to Paris, I was accompanied by not only Alain, the captain of our hosts, the rugby club with the delightful if seemingly eccentric name of Vie au Grande Aire de St Maur, but also their President and his extremely attractive and considerably younger wife to Gare du Nord, to meet the invading horde. At first, when the train pulled in, I had a nasty'thought that they'd missed the train and were still holed up in the duty-free bar of the ferry. However, it soon became apparent that, unfortunately, they'd not only caught the train but had brought most of the contents of the duty-free bar with them from the ferry. The other disembarking passengers moved quickly towards the exits, glancing apprehensively over their shoulders at a large group of wild-eyed and dishevelled lunatics cavorting in unsteady lines down the platforms, often brandishing bottles of half-consumed alcoholic beverages of every known kind and giving forth some kind of raucous tribal chant. With a sudden sinking feeling, I recognised the mental retardant leading such chant – it was our hooker, Alan (and why is this is a mandatory condition for occupants of such position?).

Madame la President watched the antics of this group with growing astonishment. "Ces, ces . gens, sont-ils votre équipe?" she asked.

"Yes," I replied weakly, "they're just showing how overjoyed they are to be in Paris" not revealing that, for many of them, this was pretty close to their normal, weekend behavioural pattern, albeit rather more exaggerated than usual.

"Mais, quesque chantent-ils?" she asked perplexedly. Having been concentrating hard on her questions, I had not taken in the content of their chorale, so it was with some dismay I realised it was a tuneless and repetitive rendering of "Wanker, wanker" with which they were greeting one of the great cultural cities of the world.

Now, generally in life, I have failed dismally to match up to those tricky occasions when an elegant, but evasive response is required, as my wife (a past master of the snide remark) was ever wont to tell me.

For once, however, fortune favoured me. "It's the English equivalent of the French word, "Vainqueur" – the winner," I said.

Madame la Président's brow cleared and she nodded, duly satisfied. "Ah, bon, c'est logique. Vainqueur – wanker. Merci. Je n'oublierais pas." And she was as good as her word, although I was not to realise quite how much so until the end of our visit.

The Saturday seemed to last for ever, especially as, for some of us at least, the Friday night ran apparently seamlessly into the following morning without any need to return to our hotel for such a mundane activity as sleeping.

Our game against St Maur being arranged for the Sunday afternoon, in the intervening period we engaged voraciously and exhaustively in the myriad delights that Paris offers touring rugby clubs. These included, it has to be admitted, any number of idiocies that, even though their instigators and participants may have considered highly original, had probably been experienced before by the citizens of Paris many times over. Whilst I tried, with no overwhelming enthusiasm, to keep these actions within certain bounds, I was hardly helped by the delighted relish with which Alain, the captain of St Maur, threw himself into joining in his guests' celebrations. I had then known Alain for over 10 years and whilst age was determinedly catching up with him, his spirit remained unfettered. I'd first met him when, as a callow youth on my first rugby trip to Paris in 1960, after all the excesses of the previous 40 hours, I packed down in the front row against him. I don't know if it's a macho thing in France, but most of the props I'd played against always wore shirts that were too small for them, with shortened sleeves and no collars, and had a weird, masochistic tendency to wear their socks rolled down to small, split-cane shin pads that only covered about half of the vulnerable bone area. They were generally about as wide as they were tall, with curiously knobbly and balding skulls but with pre and non-designer stubble and sporting an amazing range of moustaches or beards. Alain was a slight exception to the rule in that he was also taller than me but I received what I learned to recognise was the bog standard French prop's welcome. Genuinely naive to the ways of the world, I bent forward at that first scrum and he caught me with a ferocious left hook that all but closed my eye for the rest of the game. Soyez la bien venue! Vive le rugby! Vive la France!

And thus it continued; even though I'd received a similar testing examination from another French team the previous season, at each of the next scrums or line-outs, Alain or another of his team-mates would attempt to extend my education of the well-known flair and élan with which the French play rugby. And in case they missed me on those occasions, they weren't beyond having further digs in open play. Looking to the referee was of no solace; the few times when he was near and could not have failed to observe these events, he, another Frenchman, merely smiled tolerantly and moved on, pleased to see that the boys were enjoying themselves and fully entering into the spirit of things.

Fortunately, in the second row behind me, I had a minder of immense renown. Harry, a sergeant in the Metropolitan Police, quickly promised to provide assistance but also urged me to retaliate hard. "Put one on 'im," I think were his exact and elegantly articulated instructions. Thus encouraged, I duly did so at the next scrum and was pleased to note when the scrum broke up that Alain's nose had yet another bend in it and the hand that was clutching it was smeared fairly liberally with blood. Harry grunted at me approvingly and soon piled in with his own coup de grace. Alain came running round the blind side of a maul, head up, and Harry, almost absentmindedly, stuck out an elbow. Alain came to a few minutes later after the magic sponge, soaking with icy, muddy water, had been applied to his head and, for no discernible reason, to his testicles, and the game continued. I was more than a little nervous that Alain might not only take exception to this escalation of festivities but would choose to take it further. However, having stumbled groggily to his feet, he glanced across at Harry and myself and, beaming at us delightedly if a little wanly, he mumbled, "Incroyable; trés fort!"

After that first game against Alain, I made very certain that, every time I played against him subsequently, I got my retribution in first, to quote the advice of Willie-John. Indeed, by the end of our respective careers, when I was 30 and he must have been about 38, I'd have given him a decent whack before he even got onto the pitch, if I could. Alain clearly felt that this was not only acceptable, but mandatory, at least in his understanding as to how rugby should be played and, whenever I'd given him a particularly hard time in our individual contest within that of the bigger game, he'd compliment me extravagantly, shake my hand, slap me on the back and insist on buying me seemingly endless amounts of beer, wine or both after the game.

That Sunday afternoon, after the game against Vie au Grande Aire de St Maur in which the visiting English gradually came from a woefully losing position to snatch a win from under the noses of their hosts as the combined effects of beer, wine, pernod, gauloises, garlic and visits to flea-infested flophouses with middle-aged madames were run off, enormous bonhomie was enjoyed by all. Despite the sundry running hostilities that had occurred throughout the game (and which, in my experience, was the status quo when playing rugby in France) everyone was now fully involved in L'Entente Cordiale. Harry and Alain, for example, were both proudly sporting visible evidence of their commitment to their respective causes and, whilst attempting to diminish single-handedly the wine lakes that were then in existence in the Common Market, expressing undying brotherhood for one another. Such was the degree of mutual affection of all concerned that, even when the opposing alickadoos insisted on standing to make what they considered the obligatory expressions of congratulations and esteem, no-one took any offence or, more likely, notice. However, the interest of the players perceptibly quickened when, as a most unusual and much welcomed variation in such festivities, Madame la President, wearing what could best be described as the briefest of mini-skirts, stood on a chair, thus displaying a considerable amount of her undoubtedly shapely legs, and made a short congratulatory speech to the visitors. At its end, each of the visitors were encouraged to come up, in turn, to self-consciously kiss her on both cheeks, but when Alan, our hooker, finally stood before her, she stepped down, grabbed and raised his arm and triumphantly announced to the assembled multitude, "Wanker!"

Whilst Madame la President was highly gratified by the crowd's response, she must have been more than a little surprised by the rapturous reception and roars of acclaim from the assembled English.

However, as satisfying a climax as Madame la President created for that tour, the previous one had had the kiss of death on it from the start as the cast list largely consisted of mental retards. Things started badly even before the aircraft took off from the UK, when Clive, donning his well-practised air of the diplomatic smoothie, earnestly encouraged everyone to buy a half bottle of Scotch in the duty-free to give as a present to his opposite number after the match on the Sunday. Strangely enough, most followed this advice and bought a half bottle of Scotch, but without any intention of subsequent generosity to their French hosts. Dick, with his usual blunt loquacity best expressed the prevailing sentiment when he stated, "Fuck the French" and proceeded to not only down his own bottle but, when that worthy was not concentrating, half of Clive's.

In consequence, when we arrived in Paris at 10.00 pm on the Friday, a number were already in no fit state to leave the hotel to savour the city's delights. Unfortunately, that totally failed to stop them attempting to do so, and we spent nearly three hours being ejected from bar after bar because we were unable to rid ourselves of the by now wholly inebriated Dick, who insisted on following us and demanding a fresh pernod in every bar before letting it slip through his nerveless fingers to smash on the floor. What made it worse was, when each succeeding barman angrily took Dick to task, that worthy, wearing his idiot savant grin, shook his head emphatically in denial whilst the shattered shards of glass and ice lay accusingly at his feet.

Dick figured heavily on that tour, and suffered equally heavily from everyone else as a result. Having again proved a source of continual embarrassment at various bars and nightclubs on the Saturday night, he finally succumbed to excessive alcohol consumption, resulting in the rest of us having to physically transport him back to the hotel. That was the easy part – getting him up the narrow winding stairs to his hotel room was another thing altogether, especially as he was now suffering from intense and extended bouts of acute and reverberating flatulence. This was greeted with enormous outrage by those carrying him (especially those at the nether end), although I strongly suspect that some of the more evil gaseous attacks actually emanated from Dick's supporters, which they conveniently attributed to him. Certainly two of them, although bitterly voluble, seemed unable to keep a broad smile off their faces, and I have to belatedly confess that I did take the opportunity to let slip one or two of my own, but then, it was extremely exhausting lugging Dick all that way.

Having reached his room, Dick was stripped, but only to his underwear and socks as it was unanimously decided that to remove these last garments would constitute if not a crime against humanity, certainly against WHO regulations. After quickly putting him under the shower, he was then dumped, soaking wet, onto his bed, on which one of his closest friends, Chris, for reasons that even over forty years later I am totally unable to comprehend, had scattered all Dick's duty free cigarettes. Not satisfied with this contribution to our retribution, Chris then proceeded to write messages on various parts of Dick's anatomy with a blunt ball-point pen, enthusiastically if nervously aided by others; their daring and courage was but skin-deep, however, as every twitch of Dick's eyelids generated mass panic amongst his comparatively Lilliputian assailants.

The outcome was undoubtedly childish, even by the standards of the time, but it was still far too novel and subtle for the French breakfast staff, who stared in wondrous amazement at Dick the next morning, especially at the dark-blue dotted line that stretched across his forehead from ear to ear, with the words, "CUT HERE" clearly engraved above. Not having felt the inclination to wash that morning, Dick had yet to glance in the mirror and scowled in suspicion at the knowing glances, pointing fingers and varying degrees of mirth that greeted his appearance.

Given this experience, including the retaliation that Dick subsequently carved on the back of Chris on the coach to Orly Airport, plus the extensive and extraordinary events that had been packed into previous tours I'd made to Paris, I felt that I was probably overdue similar kinds of retribution and would be pushing my luck to again join such a tour. Thus, the numerous more civilised trips I've made to Paris in later years, either solo or in small parties, have been far safer and without an ever-present fear of physical or mental assault. However, I would readily admit that the ghosts of those rugby tours there are still able to elicit both internal and external mirth, albeit increasingly mistily, from my memories of those far-flung days.

THE TORTOISE & THE HARE

Quite a number aspects of playing rugby at a small rugby club have undergone considerable change over the last fifty years, at least in the UK. Probably the most noticeable and that which has had the largest and most far-reaching impact is finance. After World War 2, when money was generally in very short supply for everyone and the UK and much of Europe were teetering on the edge of bankruptcy, all sports here were run in a very much make-and-mend fashion. In the UK, I'd be very surprised if the by far and away most wealthy sport proved not to be Association Football, or soccer. On thinking about it though, maybe it would be more accurate to state that, with so many of its clubs, both professional and amateur, continuously flirting with financial oblivion, soccer only generates the greatest amount of income each year, overall. Certainly, it needs to, if only to pay the grossly inflated wage structures it has somehow ludicrously managed to tie itself into at the highest level. How can anyone justify the payment of over £300,000 a week to individuals to simply kick a ball around, individuals who often act like spoilt brats? Paying such an amount to them on just an annual basis would, in any balanced society, be excessive in the extreme. Not that I blame the individuals concerned, as distasteful as I often find a number of them; if someone is daft enough to offer you such exorbitant wealth, who wouldn't take it?

What I find curious, though, is the speed at which the financial benefits that the top soccer players can earn has ramped up. It was only back in 1963 that, due to the determination and sheer bloody-mindedness of George Eastham, the then all pervasive "Retain-

and-Transfer" system imposed by the clubs was largely ruled to be unreasonable by the courts and did indeed, as claimed by George Eastham and the Professional Footballers' Association, constitute an unlawful constraint of trade. One of the more loathed restraints of this system, certainly by the footballers, was the £20 a week maximum wage. Given current market practice and headlined contract claims, that seems like a damn sight more than just 50 years ago.

Rugby Union, by comparison, has never really suffered from such problems, the principal reason being that there was no organised professional side to the game until 1995. Even then, with both rugby codes being (and likely to remain) minority sports, albeit probably influential beyond their size, the financial rewards available to professional rugby players is but petty cash compared to that earned by the top soccer players.

However, there is a curious dichotomy between professional soccer and its amateur form. Logically, one would expect the amateur game to meld seamlessly into its professional relation, providing a continuous source of new, young players. That certainly happens, but amateur soccer has long been the poor relation amongst the more populous sports in the UK. From my admittedly less than overwhelming experiences, amateur soccer clubs can often exist for only a few years; they have little if any common base to bind the players together. Very few of them are built up and organised such that they buy or even rent their own clubhouses; similarly, a considerable percentage of them run just the one team and, if a player feels he's not getting enough game-time, he'll leave and join another club. When I left school and joined my "Old Boys" club, for example, we had a number of players who'd abandoned playing soccer and, despite their ongoing assertion that soccer remained the better game, switched to playing Rugby Union. Why? Because of the strong, social relationships that existed between the individual rugby players, inclusive of their bonding to their club. It was best explained to me by a close friend who, although he had begrudgingly played rugby with me at school, switched back to playing soccer as soon as he left. However, after less than three years, he reluctantly returned to rugby. Since the two of us had remained in close social touch in this intervening period, I was not wholly surprised. As he explained, as much as he loved the actual game of soccer, all the peripheral aspects were at best, well, shoddy (as he put it). The games were always played locally and on a local council pitch that had virtually always seen better days. If there were any changing facilities, these were basic at the very least; the Rolls-Royce of these constructions would be a largish, wooden gardening shed in which two teams and the referee would be supposed to change. Sometimes, there would be a couple of hand-basins and, now and again, wonder of wonders, maybe a couple of shower-heads. Toilets? Who needed toilets; you went before you left home and then kept it bottled up until you got home again. If you couldn't wait that long you went behind either the shed or a convenient tree. Anything more serious and you were a dead man.

This meant, I was told, that just about everyone turned up ready changed, or did so in the back of a car. Referees would universally adopt this practice on a matter of health and safety. Disagreements with their decisions were not only the norm but almost universally expected; but these could regularly escalate into semi-coherent and extremely heated arguments, not irregularly leading to punch-ups involving not only those on the pitch but a few incensed supporters, as well. Given the number of not wholly amicable promises to "see you after the game" from players aggrieved by referees' decisions not in their favour, It was hardly surprising that it was not uncommon for referees to blow the final whistle when, close enough to the actual time, they had manoeuvred themselves into fairly easy sprinting distances from their cars.

And then, when the game was over, they'd all gather their tents like Arabs and silently steal away. Well, not quite. They'd exchange parting messages and enquiries as to availability for next week's match, and that was it. Home for a hot bath and tea with the missus, not exactly a consummation devoutly to be wished, especially when, every so often, she'd been taken to an evening out at the local rugby club to meet his old school chums. Hence the conversion back to rugby union, albeit primarily for social reasons and comparative peace in our time at home.

Thus, having no professional league to which to aspire or which might be induced to provide some kind of financial support, however miniscule, rugby players had to rely upon their own efforts and ambitions if they wished to improve and better enjoy their game, however confusing and illogical it might be to outsiders. And often to themselves, it has to be admitted. When my father was first commanded by my mother to take me with him as a condition of his being granted leave of absence for the latter half of each winter Saturday, I can remember very few clubs having premises of their own. Mostly, my father and his team-mates would change in pubs, at least back in the late 1940s. By the early 1950s, by hard work and a consummate desire to obtain their own, far more suitable and bespoke premises, a fair number had managed to raise sufficient funds to purchase what, quite often at first sight, would seem to be pretty in-appropriate buildings for use as clubhouses. But this very situation seemed to act as yet a further spur to create almost a home from home. Raffles were held; dances were organised; treasure hunts became a regular Sunday outing for not just players but their entire immediate families. By these and other often bizarre methods, further funds were raised to bring what had originally been dubiously suitable buildings to rugby clubhouses that their members came to treasure, however one-eyed such appreciation may have been to third parties. Indeed, it was often the incongruity of these converted old houses, dance schools, decommissioned old pubs and even abandoned police stations that made them so heart-warmingly personal and individual to both their owners and to most visitors. The bars were often quixotic little hide-aways; and finding the toilet could be akin to a trek in the dark through some haunted house, amusing if you were not stooped over with a full-to-bursting bladder but both painful and terrifying if otherwise.

Creating such clubhouses infused a wonderful spirit of comradeship amongst the players. These clubhouses were ours; we had sweated blood and tears for them and given up not just considerable time and effort in communal projects to get them up and running, but had often contributed whatever donations we could afford. Not only that but none of us, even the stars in the first fifteens of small clubs, ever received any financial compensation to play for their clubs. We had to not only pay our subscriptions and match fees, but for all our kit. We didn't get free-bees like club jerseys, let alone track suits or shell suits and the like. Track suits and shell suits? What the hell were they? The only players in small clubs that I can remember, back in the late 1950s through early 1970s, that were supported financially in any way were the university students that had been persuaded to return home at weekends to play for their clubs. When that happened, they were let-off match fees and were also reimbursed for their travelling costs for getting to the matches, home or away, but nothing else.

As a result, Saturday afternoons during the rugby season were the highlight of the week to us all, and matches played away were prized above all. Unless you were newly affianced or married that is. For the other players at each end of the social spectrum, it was a different story. From the maladroit youngsters as yet without temporary let alone permanent female partners at one end to the old lags treasuring their last few seasons before the combination of disintegrating bodies and increasing domestic demands of their wives at the other, away matches had attractions that, these days, are only matched by the siren tones of TV adverts for Mediterranean cruises. And the further away these matches, the better, as nobody could then reasonably expect them to get home too early, like at 10 pm. Which, in turn, meant more pubs, both old favourites and new recommendations, could be visited on the way back.

Here, it has to be admitted that, under today's laws against drinking and driving, what happened on all these away trips was extremely stupid and probably exceptionally hazardous. There is no gainsaying that fact, but, at the time, no such laws existed. There were also far, far fewer cars on the road and the cars in which we travelled usually had much less power than those available today. In addition, a substantial percentage of these cars were either pre-World War 2 or constructed almost immediately after. And if you owned anything newer than that, you'd certainly never be fool enough to bring it to the rugby club on Saturday and then, to your horror and chagrin, be forced into volunteering it for transporting up to six or seven passengers all with a history of and delight in buffoonery and a range of other mad antics. However, it did happen at least once to my knowledge.

We had a first fifteen match against Colchester, about forty miles away if you took the better roads of the A127, A130 and A12. As usual, we had gathered at our clubhouse in Leigh-on-Sea but discovered that Malcolm, our highly erudite and extremely organised captain, was not there. Instead, his vice-captain, Ray, advised us that Malcolm had some business to perform in London that morning and would be making his own way to Colchester. Ray then checked us all in and organised our departure for Colchester. As was normal, there wasn't really sufficient room for us all in the cars available, and we grumblingly fitted ourselves into the three cars present, consisting of Brian's beat-up Morris Minor and two other similar-sized vehicles whose make and owners' identities have all been erased from my memory by the passage of time. We were also less than happy that we'd have to squeeze Malcolm into one of these cars for the return journey, as Malcolm was a very muscular 6'3" or more.

When we arrived at Colchester, surprise, surprise, Malcolm had got their first. What's more, he arrived there in a spanking new car, the acquisition of which had been the business in London he had had to conclude before joining us. And what a new car! It was a brand new, peacock-blue Austin Healey 3000! And it was utterly, gob-smacking, heart-achingly beautiful.

Now, it wasn't as if our club didn't have other members who could boast wonderful, envy-inducing vehicles. Ian, for example, a former captain, possessed the first real E-type Jaguar that any of us had seen, but Ian was passé. Firstly, he'd already retired from playing; secondly, he was now married, to the stunningly attractive and intelligent Bubbles; and, thirdly, well, he was at least 35 and thus clearly over the hill and stumbling down the other side. Whereas Malcolm was still one of us, mostly impecunious and, sadly, almost universally without the all-important je ne sais pas quoi to attract young, nubile, sexually voracious females. So, when we arrived at Colchester and there was this absolutely marvellous motor car sat there in front of us, its chrome all sparkling and, its roof being down, with thick, cream, leather upholstery, we all drooled over it. All except Brian.

Don't misunderstand me; Brian wasn't sulking with envy or a closet communist being forced out into the open. Brian truly cared little if anything for either extreme wealth or its manifestations. But he was a mischievous bastard who delighted in coming out of left field to confound, amaze and embarrass people just to show them he could do so. He said nothing whatsoever at the time, just went about getting changed for the match with a private little smile on his face. If any of us had noticed his demeanour, we might have guessed that a devious plan was being hatched behind his smile, but the rest of us were far too engrossed in Malcolm's car to wonder at Brian's seemingly content silence.

What happened during the game I cannot remember; and it has no relevance whatsoever to what followed. We enjoyed the normal hospitality that we would have expected except that, at about the time people were glancing at their watches to see how long it'd be before we left for the journey home, Brian's evil machinations were first floated gently and apparently innocently into the discussions. "Well," asked Brian in his slightly high-pitched voice, "now we've got an extra seat for the journey back, who's going to go with Malcolm?"

On the face of it, this was a perfectly valid question, but Brian was simply casting some bread upon the waters. There was a moment's silence while we all digested the import of his question and then the younger bloods in the team all began looking to Malcolm to see if they could obtain his patronage. All except one that is. Bobby, our scrumhalf, and therefore automatically viewed as a cunning, Machiavellian and underhand sneak, had worked out, from the very moment he first saw the Austin Healey with Malcolm sitting alone inside, that this presented him with a golden opportunity to travel home in comfort and unrivalled style. Of course, another advantage of making such a pre-emptive move was Bobby's clearly calculated degree of superiority that it would bestow on him over the rest of us returning in the alternative transport of clapped-out bangers. This was at once evident from Bobby's smug smile when Malcolm confirmed to us all that Bobby had already reserved the passenger seat in his car.

Into this mixed atmosphere of envy and disgruntlement shown by the younger players and the amusement of the three other drivers and a few older players, Brian then placed his hook. "Don't know what all the fuss is about," he remarked disdainfully, "Malcolm won't get home any faster than the rest of us."

This was such a self-evidently ludicrous remark, even for Brian, that we all gazed at him with varying degrees of dis-belief. Only Malcolm didn't rise to the bait because, being probably naturally confident in the undoubtedly superior performance of his new car, he could afford to give Brian a tolerant smile. A number of voices then ridiculed Brian's claim and he waited patiently for these to die down before he made a first tug on his hook. "It's true," averred dismissively, in his high tenor, "in fact, I'll bet that I can get back to our clubhouse in my car before Malcolm can in his new whizz-bang."

Again, there was a moment's incredulity before a number of his team-mates groped for the bait including (most importantly to Brian) Malcolm, determined to dismiss this slur regarding his new car's capabilities. "What d'you mean, you'll bet your crappy old Morris Minor can get back home before my Austin Healey? How much?"

Brian made another tug on his line. "Ten bob."

"Ten bob?" responded Malcolm contemptuously, "I wouldn't get out of bed for that."

"All right then," squeaked Brian, "a fiver?"

At this point it should be remembered that five pounds was a not inconsiderable sum of money back then in the early 1960s. As a senior articled clerk, I was then earning £4 a week, less deductions; a pint of bitter cost about half-a-crown, or two shillings and sixpence (that's 12.5p in decimalised sterling); and ten cigarettes, if my memory is correct, were about the same. So Brian's increased challenge was not to be sniffed at. But Malcolm was not going to allow Brian's boastful presumption to go for as little as that. "Make it ten quid," he threw back, "and you've got a bet."

Brian wasn't fazed in the slightest. "Tell you what," he offered, "let's make it a barrel of beer, a firkin, to be bought back at the club, by the loser."

A firkin was just about the smallest barrel of beer that would be supplied by a brewer, and contained 72 pints. As such, it would cost about £9 to buy a barrel at our own clubhouse. Malcolm shrugged with complete indifference; if it had cost £50 he would have accepted the bet, so confident was he that he couldn't possibly lose it. "But," insisted Brian, "it's subject to three conditions."

At this, all our antennae, slumbering peacefully until then, pricked up, especially given Brian's known inclinations for mischief. A hush fell as we all listened carefully. Also, Malcolm was immediately more circumspect in his evaluation of the sense of taking Brian's bet. "What conditions?" he asked carefully.

"First," came the response, "rather than going home the way we came up, on the new dual carriageways, we go back on the old cross-country route, through Tolle shunt D'Arcy, Maldon, Bicknacre, Woodham Ferrers and Battlesbridge."

This was an understandable condition as, although this route would be probably over 10 miles shorter, the two cars would have to travel along some fairly narrow, winding roads such as the B1026, A414 and A132. Even so, there were enough stretches that were both straight and wide enough for Malcolm to roar past Brian. Malcolm considered this proposition minutely, looking for the hidden catches that he (and the rest of us) suspected Brian had devised. Finding none, he nodded briefly. "OK."

"Second," Brian proposed, "I want a five minute start."

Malcolm frowned at this. Surely such an advantage contradicted Brian's underlying claim that he could get back quicker than Malcolm. However, so caught up by now in the challenge was Malcolm and so keen his desire to wipe Brian's face in the mire that, after briefly mulling over the pros and cons in his mind, Malcolm again acceded. "OK, but what's the third condition?" he enquired.

"Both cars have got to have a full load," replied Brian, with a totally bland expression on his face.

We all stopped and thought about this, realising that, somehow, Brian had created some kind of trap for Malcolm but without having the faintest idea of what it might be. Why would Brian, driving his old Morris Minor with its three bald tyres, want to have at least four passengers with him for the journey home? Surely it would be far more beneficial if he drove home alone, thus reducing materially the weight of the car? Malcolm glared at Brian suspiciously whilst he and the rest of us examined this third condition for nearly a couple of minutes. Finally, reluctantly, even though he felt sure there was some hidden snare that he'd missed, Malcolm nodded and thrust out his hand. Brian grasped it at once with what looked remarkably like a evilly triumphant grin, and elected to take with him four of the same five passengers who'd travelled up with him, including myself, to constitute his allotted load home.

Shortly afterwards, everyone's interest now being fully focussed on the race home (and in subsequently helping the winner to consume his prize of 72 pints of bitter), we picked up our kit and, saying goodbye to our hosts, congregated in the car park. Brian and Malcolm having agreed upon an independent adjudicator who'd ensure that Malcolm wouldn't start out until at least five minutes after Brian had left, we chosen four then piled into Brian's Morris Minor with him. Tyres spinning as they desperately sought grip, Brian gunned the engine (as much as it could be gunned) and we swerved out of the car park and onto the back roads home.

It was then, in between making regular glances out of the rear window for the onrushing headlights of what would doubtless be Malcolm's charging Austin Healey, that Brian gave out his instructions and we came to understand the fiendish nature of his scheme. When we climbed into his car, I don't believe any of us gave him a snowball's chance in hell of succeeding but, once he'd divulged his plans, we probably upgraded his chances to about fifty/fifty.

After we'd been gone just over fifteen minutes or so along the pitch-black country roads, with only the occasional vehicle coming the other way, we first began to catch flashes of headlights behind us. Then, as the Austin Healey ate up the ground between the two vehicles and we were halfway along a straight section of road, the headlights came barrelling into full view. We instantly knew it was Malcolm as he flashed his headlights on and off full-beam two or three times to signal to the tortoise of the arrival of the hare. But was Brian dismayed at this turn of events, even though he must have known, in his heart of hearts, that it was bound to happen? Not a bit of it; he'd not only planned on it but had fully thought out his defensive strategy to combat it. As the Austin Healey came charging up behind us, with Malcolm leaning on its horn, Brian bellowed out, "Now!" and we executed the instructions he'd given us earlier. At the same time as he edged the Morris Minor over to the middle of the road, straddling the white line, the rest of us opened our doors wide. Faced suddenly with a car that, being double its previous width, now blocked up nearly the whole road, Malcolm was forced to jam on his brakes, no doubt accompanied by some extremely choice language.

And thus we continued, for mile upon mile, all the way to the outskirts of Leigh. When there was nothing coming the other way, Brian would hold the Morris Minor to the centre of the road, no matter how much Malcolm sat on his horn in increasing fury and desperation and swerved the Austin Healey from side to side in the hope of finding a wider patch of road through which he might gun it through. On the very few occasions when a car did come the other way, on such a dark night as this the reflections of its on-coming headlights gave Brian a fair degree of prior warning such that, when it hove into actual sight, he would command us to shut the doors and demurely move his car to the left of the road. Then, as soon as the other car had passed us, Brian would re-employ his defensive strategy and Malcolm would be left powerless to overtake.

Believe it or not, this procession continued all the way back to our clubhouse in Leigh. Indeed, by the time we arrived there, this procession had been increased by a number of other cars. Two of them were the rest of our original convoy and, whilst those inside these vehicles later confirmed to us the delight, admiration and immense amusement they had derived from Brian's cunning, God alone knew what the people in the other cars thought about it all, poor sods.

Anyway, once back in our own clubhouse, Malcolm proved himself to be the gentleman he would undoubtedly become in the future, if not held back, in the interim, by such obvious miscreants and ne'er-do-wells as the rest of us. He paid up without the slightest quibble, and even with the vestige of a rueful smile.

Didn't bring the Austin Healey to many more away matches, though.

SAVE THE LAST DANCE FOR ME

At first consideration, you must be thinking, what has dancing got to do with rugby clubs? Why would there be a chapter about dancing in a book of this nature? To be honest, it's a pretty intangible link but it's true to say that, except when playing away, or on tour, when the primary object was always to consume as much alcoholic refreshment as was available and to behave as disgracefully as possible without causing too much offence, going to a local hop was almost always how your Saturday evening would end up. Of course, you also hoped you'd be lucky there and would pull a member of the opposite sex. If not (and far more likely if not almost certain), you'd finish up at just before or after midnight at an Indian or Chinese restaurant with a host of other unsuccessful and disappointed would-be Romeos.

When I was first encouraged to join those other individuals with whom I'd played rugby that afternoon and then spent the early evening carousing in our clubhouse before accompanying them to a local dance, it was almost exclusively to what was generally a pretty unappetising hall adjoining or even above a local pub. But the lack of elegance in the surroundings never even crossed our minds; we couldn't have given a toss. We went there for two things only; more booze (and up to midnight, rather than up to just 10.30 pm) and to try and persuade some voluptuous and, hopefully, determinedly sexually hungry young female to accompany you somewhere private for energetic and exhausting physical interplay. And where, exactly, would this "somewhere private" location actually be? Sadly, this was seldom if ever determined or arranged in advance as the likelihood of actually both finding such a female and then getting her to leave the dance with you were pretty limited, almost to the point of invisibility in fact.

Why our level of success in this objective was so abysmal was something that, somehow, we never managed to understand. This is particularly surprising when, looking back over the years, the answer is so obvious. Why would any young lady be attracted to a male clearly the worse for wear when there were far more better dressed, better behaved and more interesting alternatives available? Also, it never occurred to us (or at least, to me) that the female attendees at the dance did not go there with the same objectives as ourselves, that they actually enjoyed dancing for the sake of it. What? Surely not; they actually enjoyed jiggling and jerking their bodies in such un-coordinated movements around the dance floor?

Nevertheless, hope does indeed spring eternal and Saturday night after Saturday night we would pursue the Golden Fleece, with just about exactly the same level of success every week. Afterwards, we would traipse off, semi-disconsolately, to whichever local restaurant would still be open and prepared to continue supplying further "refreshments", typically in the shape of bottled beer. Although both Chinese and Indian restaurants would be available, it was more often that the Indian variety would be chosen since the Chinese would be more concerned that such late night entrants would be both unruly and highly likely to upset their already seated clientele. A pretty fair estimation at that. The Indian restaurants had far less scruples in this regard and, once inside, a fresh contest would usually occur between those of us that found ourselves seated around a communal table – who could eat the hottest curry.

Why this fascination existed (and, according to my two sons, exists to this very day), I have never been able to work out. Given that so many of my peers have, over the years, like me, gradually lowered their proclaimed capabilities to enjoy the hottest of curries to the much milder attractions of a Korma, a Pasanda, a Mughlai or a Rogan Josh, I can only assume that their earlier boasts of being able to consume, without any qualms or subsequent physical suffering, a Vindaloo or a Phall were just that; the machismo of youth. Certainly I can remember on any number of occasions, sitting with three equally inane companions at a table in an Indian restaurant in the very early hours of the morning, with the sweat pouring down my face whilst assuring all and sundry that, "No, it isn't that hot; I've had much hotter than this."

None of my companions would contradict such evident nonsense since they would be in exactly the same way; it had become somehow a matter of honour not to admit defeat and opt for the easy way out. The only ones present that could discern the true state of affairs were the restaurant staff, who'd stand in the doorway to the kitchen and try hard not to snigger at this seemingly never-ending stupidity from the would-be descendants of the Raj.

And not only were the resulting paybacks almost immediate. Hot flushes, sweaty foreheads, runny noses, semi-closed and paralysed vocal chords would occur after only a few mouthfuls. Not only that, but your tongue and taste-buds suffered such severe burn-out that the delicacy of any side dish ordered would be completely overwhelmed. But the worst of it was the horror and distaste with which your body reacted to this demonic consumable being forced upon it. The stomach pains and resulting farts that would cause such discomfort throughout the following hours of darkness (and the terrifying concern, after each fart, as you were jerked into consciousness, lest it had not been a dry one) were as nothing compared to the severe anal burning that would plague you until almost the following midday.

Many's the time when, catching an early train on the Monday to go to work in London that I found it nigh on impossible to sit still and composed on my seat. It truly felt as if the proverbial red-hot poker had been shoved up my arse, au Edward II. On occasions like that and when the train was full and an elderly gentleman (anybody over 40) was unable to find a seat, I'd willingly clamber awkwardly to my feet to seek relief from the pain behind me.

However, enough of this diversion. Dancing, then, was never something that I or most of my male companions ever cared for greatly; it was merely something that had to be endured to attain our greater objectives. Not surprisingly, therefore, I don't recall one occasion when any of us were approached by a young lady and asked if we'd like to dance. That simply wasn't done; and even if it was, I strongly doubt that any of the young ladies that went to the dances described above would have been desperate enough to approach me or my friends. The unattached females at those dances would far rather dance with each other than encourage hoi polloi from the local rugby club.

As my friends and I grew older and acquired a certain level of understanding of the ways of the world, we decided that, if we couldn't score at these externally promoted dances, then maybe we should organise our own dances at the rugby club. At first, these were a good deal less than wholly successful. True, we had a fairly suitable area for dancing, a bar and any number of single men, but for reasons that were not immediately apparent to us, very few single women. Oh, sure, these dances attracted up to about twenty females but these were all spoken for, being the wives, fiancées or girlfriends of the club members concerned. I'm sure they found these dances most agreeable since they were ensured of dancing partners the whole evening. What's more, this would be dancing to a real live band, not to the eccentric choices of a local weirdo that proffered his services as a disc jockey.

Our first attempts to address this in-balance of the sexes was to turn to the known Letharios in our midst. First there was Clive, a brash and highly confident individual who was absolutely positive that he was wholly irresistible to women. Sadly, and to the immense irritation of the rest of us, this often proved to be the case. Then there was Barry, whose character was at completely the other end of the spectrum. Barry was one of those men who are annoyingly naturally elegant whatever they wear, with lovely manners and an impish smile, who also seldom found himself without female admirers. So, these two worthies would be sent off to do a round of the local pubs to see if they could locate and entice young, attractive, unaccompanied females to our dances. Amazingly, they were successful, even if only moderately so.

We then gradually got onto a roll and, as success bred success, our dances grew more and more popular until, in the end, we had to turn away would be attendees. The rugby club could only take about 250 people and, when full, the room on the dance floor would be minimal. Thus, when we approached the standing room only point, the message would be passed to those manning the door (not that they needed much advice, since the door opened immediately onto the dance floor) to go to Plan B. Any additional, unaccompanied males would be sorrowfully advised that, sincere apologies but we were full, so be sure to come early next time. For unaccompanied females, the message would be just ever so slightly different. They would also be advised that the dance was full but, when they expressed disappointment, be invited to look around the door to see for themselves. This would usually prove the clincher; seeing the mass of people jammed together on the dance floor, writhing and singing along with the music, nearly always engendered an almost desperate need in the girls concerned to be allowed in. And naturally, being the undoubted good fellows that they were, the guardians at the door allowed themselves to be persuaded to bend the rules and let them in. Just this once, mind.

This gradually increasing number on the dance floor made it virtually impossible to continue with the more abandoned, leg-shaking, arms-waving gyrations that had been so evident earlier in the evening. Instead, the band gradually introduced more and more, slow, smoochy numbers until, ultimately, under the increasingly dim light, the floor space appeared occupied by a hydra-headed, slow-moving mythical creature. Additional to the ever decreasing space available for dancing, this was caused by the fact that, by this time of the night, the band was just about knackered. Back then, in the mid and late sixties, when a pint of beer was under two shillings (or 10p in new money), the four members of the band that we booked exclusively over this period were paid a total of £20.00 for the night, starting at about 7.45 pm and finishing at about midnight, with two short breaks of about fifteen minutes each. Oh, and all the beer they could drink. This, and the steadily increasing temperature within the rugby club caused by the excessive number of bodies being crammed inside, meant that by about 11.00 p.m. the band was not only getting exhausted but, additional to being three sheets to the wind, were extremely hot and sweaty. In self-defence, therefore, their earlier exuberance and sometimes spectacularly acrobatic movements that accompanied their playing had to be reined in.

Not that the dancers minded and any amount of surreptitious fondling probably took place, pressed close together as they all were. Certainly, I never heard any of the men present complain about being sexually harassed. Come to think of it, and rather more curious, nor from the women, either.

However, as enjoyable and successful as these dances became, there was a down-side. Becoming as hot as it did inside the rugby club, many of its windows were opened to let the heat out. Unfortunately, not only was the heat let out but also the noise of the band and this was not to the amusement and liking of some of our neighbours. This led to presumably irate phone calls being made to the local nick and, initially, to a slightly apologetic visit from the boys in blue. However, once their increasingly eye-popping surveillance around the front door of the scene inside the rugby club had registered, we began to realise that by about 11.30 p.m. at first one and then more police cars would be stationary at nearby kerbs. Obviously, two and two had been added together and the answer could be a healthy increase in drink driving prosecutions and accompanying fines.

Drink driving legislation was introduced in the UK in 1967. Before then, not that many people (at least of my then age) were sufficiently sensible or social minded to regard drinking and driving as being particularly out of the ordinary. Whilst that was no excuse, there were not only far fewer cars on the roads in those days but those that were generally had nothing like the power that even the smallest vehicle has today. For example, my first car, a pre WW2 Austin Seven Chummy, had only a 747 cc engine that developed just 10 bhp and, downhill, with a following wind and a good deal of luck, could roar away at 45 mph. Well, almost. By comparison, one of the smallest modern cars currently available is the Peugeot 208, which has a 1.2 litre engine that develops 82 bhp and a top speed of well over 120 mph.

In consequence, our attitudes to drinking and driving were far more cavalier and irresponsible and, although this disgraceful, underhand behaviour by the police was considered not just mean-spirited but wholly unethical, common sense prevailed, prompted by the manner in which the band executed their own departure from the rugby club. Although their leader and lead guitarist, Tim, was generally wholly wasted by the end of the dance, as were the bass guitarist, drummer and keyboard player, he had already put in place his own cunning plan. Just before midnight, Tim's father would arrive with his Ford Transit van and, as soon as the witching hour had struck, he would dis-assemble all the band's musical instruments and gear and load them into the back of his van. He'd then return and gently shepherd Tim and his mates out to the van and, having helped them conquer the north face of the van's back steps, would jauntily wave good night to us before carefully driving away.

These dances became such joyful and much-anticipated social gatherings that I was wholly unprepared for what I'd assumed would be their doppelgangers in southern Ireland.

Back in the mid-1960s, I'd got into the habit of joining two of my closer friends, Bobby and Malcolm, for lunch, two or three times a week, at the Shakespeare's Head on the corners of Carnaby and Great Marlborough Streets, just behind The London Palladium. Bobby and I were still articled clerks but Malcolm, being older, far more diligent and probably intelligent as well, had already passed his finals and had ascended to the eminence of a Member of the Institute of Chartered Accountants in England and Wales. One lunchtime, Malcolm brought with him Declan, a colleague who hailed from very southern Ireland, from Bantry. Declan was very much the Irishman of fable, an extremely hail-fellow-well-met character, the Irish Rover with the twinkling eye who'd clearly kissed the Blarney Stone at least a dozen times.

Over the next few weeks we all met up with Declan again on a number of occasions and, once he'd got to know us all better, he put a proposal to us just before Easter that seemed immensely interesting and attractive.

Over here in England, Declan played rugby for London Irish – who else? But back in Ireland, he was a stalwart supporter of and player for his local club in Bantry. This was a club not dissimilar to thousands of other around the world, a small, unpretentious and unremarkable but extremely hospitable and friendly gathering of local individuals with but one objective on every Saturday during the rugby season – to kick shit out of whomever were the opposing side that day and then to embrace them fondly in the bar afterwards. Plus, of course, to thoroughly re-hydrate themselves after the enormous exertions of the now concluded afternoon's battle. As a quick aside at this point, I've never really understood this modern habit of sending on herds of water boys at seemingly every possible stoppage during a game. Nobody's going to suffer irreparable physical damage if they haven't swigged down a few mouthfuls of water during a game every five or so minutes, for Christ's sake; you do all your re-hydrating after the game, in the bar. At least, we did. Anyway, Declan's proposal was related to his club back in Bantry. Apparently, a lot of its younger members, like so many other young Irish men and women over the time since the Great Hunger of the 1840s had emigrated, temporarily or permanently, mostly the latter. Like Declan himself. As a result, Declan's club, what with recent injuries to those players still living in and around Bantry during recent skirmishes with other clubs, plus this draining away of its younger, up-and-coming bloods, was suffering a horrendously miserable season and had not won a match to date. In consequence, a call had gone out to all its absent sons to come to the club's aid for the forthcoming match against their nearest and deadliest rivals, especially as they, by comparison, were unbeaten so far that season.

Declan not only made immediate plans to return to Bantry for that weekend and make himself available for this crucial defence of his home town's honour but had also been asked to see if he could bolster the team's strengths through the recruitment of a few ringers to accompany him. Having enjoined Declan in a number of boisterous discussions about our own recent exploits for our own rugby club in which our individual skills, bravery and brilliance no doubt figured increasingly to the fore, Declan therefore asked if we'd be interested in turning out for Bantry. Not only that, but before we could quickly withdraw some of our vainfully expressed achievements, he earnestly assured us it wouldn't cost us a penny. Not that we'd get paid anything, you understand, but all travelling and hotel expenses would be met by his club and, of course, we'd be entertained like visiting royalty.

Malcolm, Bobby and I blinked and quickly glanced at one another. This was something rather different; but how much trust could we place in Declan's assurance that all our expenses would be paid? A spot of horse-trading then followed with the three of us agreeing, in principle, to accompany Declan to Bantry provided that he not only purchased, in advance, all the necessary travel tickets but that we received, also in advance, written proof that whatever hotel we stayed at had confirmed our reservations and that they would be looking solely to Declan to meet the resulting costs.

As a result, one Friday evening after work, some three weeks later, the four of us set off by train from London to Pembroke, where we took the ferry to Rosslare at about midnight. Malcolm, Bobby and I travelled light, with not just our rugby gear in a carry-on but also some spare clothes. By comparison, Declan seemed prepared for a month in Antarctica. Additional to his rugby kit, he brought with him a pretty sizeable suitcase, but then, he was probably taking presents home for his family.

Once in the Republic, another train journey followed, from Rosslare to Cork, where we transferred to an extremely antiquated and crowded bus at just after 7.00 am that meandered its way to Bantry. All in all, the bulk of this journey took not far short of 17 hours so we arrived at Cork at about midday on Saturday, with kick-off just two hours away. Given the time it took the bus to get to our ultimate destination, with the driver insistent on not only helping off his passengers at every tiny village on his route but also nipping in to the nearest bar for sustenance, by the time we actually arrived at Bantry, Malcolm, Bobby and I had all become more than a little concerned that we'd ever get there on time.

By comparison, Declan showed neither impatience nor apprehension as the hands on the old clock on the bus ticked inexorably around towards the scheduled kick-off time. "To be sure, there's absolutely no need to worry," he assured us, "It's certain they'll be holdin' up the start 'til we arrive." He glanced questioningly at the clock and opined, "In fact, we should even be able to get in a couple o' swift halves before we take to the field."

Thus comforted, we were in a comparatively happy frame of mind when we rolled into Bantry. This was just as well because, as wonderfully scenic as Bantry and its surrounding countryside and bay were, these delights rather lose their charm if, when you arrive, it's not just pissing down but, judging by the size of the puddles that surrounded the bus stop and, indeed, just about saturated the whole length of the only road in Bantry, had been doing so for a very, very, long time.

Declan then introduced us to our hotel which, rather appropriately, just like us, had over-presented itself; it was a simple and extremely basic bed-and-breakfast establishment. This, however, did not concern us in the slightest. Even though our rooms were Spartan in the extreme and had clearly provided inspirations for Phiz in Dickens' books, we had no plans to spend time there except when it became absolutely necessary to find a bed. And as for the lack of a bar, why, we were next door to a pub and we'd also spotted a number of other promising looking hostelries along the street.

Having off-loaded our spare clothing, we were picked up by an old friend of Declan's who transported us and our kit in an ancient pick-up truck that was clearly used normally in the garage trade. Thankfully, it was but a short ride to the rugby club and we spent it perched somewhat disconsolately on old wheels and other spare vehicle parts in the open back of the truck, huddled against the rain.

The match that followed was not one I cherish. Any resemblance between it and the games of rugby I'd played elsewhere was purely coincidental. As far as we, the visiting foreigners, were concerned, it was a pure exercise in tribal warfare, conveniently disguised as a rugby match. If the events that transpired on that pitch had occurred in a city centre, like Cork or Dublin, the Guarda would have been called to break it up and cart us all away on any number of charges. Problem was, as I found out in the bar afterwards, a large number of the visiting team were Guardai themselves. We therefore drew little sympathy there and, after Malcolm had his nose broken and Bobby lost a tooth, we managed to put two and two together and start returning fire with fire.

Now, normally in those far-off days, amateur rugby press reports often claimed when covering an away fixture that had been lost, that the result had been due to star players being unavailable through injury, a long and tiring journey, a wholly unsuitable pitch, all the luck in the game going the opposition's way and an unsympathetic referee. Or even a combination of all the above. Then, if you'd lost 50-0, it was entirely against the run of play and because of a number of dodgy refereeing decisions; honestly, folks, a draw would have far better reflected the run of play.

Well, even though Bantry were playing at home, some of us had experienced a tiring journey to get there and we played on a real bog of a pitch. Even so, it has to be said that the real visitors were the better side, possibly excepting in some of the individual punch-ups that broke out almost continually throughout the match and in which, after going behind initially, Bantry truly fought back to obtain an overall draw. That's what both sets of players convivially agreed in the bar afterwards anyway, and what everyone present, including the referee and the supporters, appeared to consider the most important statistic to result from the match. The actual result? Bantry lost but, as to the score, I haven't a clue, although we seemed to line up behind our posts a hell of a sight more often than they did.

Malcolm, Bobby and I then looked forward with great relish to the evening evolving into the kind of festivities that Declan had promised and which, to be truthful, were probably the single largest factor in our decision to accompany him back to Bantry. We had nothing extravagant in mind, just a slow and gentle start that would hopefully accelerate into a significantly uproarious night. But somehow, it didn't go down that path in the way we expected. At around 7.00 pm, the Bantry lads started slipping away and, thus left increasingly in the majority, the visitors had a brief conference and then determined to head back home, via a number of not unknown hostelries on the way. At just after 8.00 pm, there were thus few others left in the rather ramshackle building that served as the rugby club except Malcolm, Bobby and myself, plus Declan and a few other local stalwarts.

This, however, did not faze Declan in the slightest. "Right, lads," he addressed us cheerfully, "time to be gettin' changed and havin' our evenin' meal."

The evening meal sounded like a reasonable idea, but why would we need to get changed, for God's sake? "Wasn't I tellin' yer?" asked Declan in some surprise, "To go to the dance, and yer surely don't want to be a-goin' there lookin' like that, do yer?"

"What dance?" we responded in unison.

"It's the monthly dance they're holdin' at the school," said Declan. "Surely, yer knew about that?"

"No," stated Malcolm, "how on earth could we?"

"No? Ah well, it's no problem anyway," observed Declan. "We'll be gettin' you back to the hotel so yer can change and then we'll be goin' out for a meal."

And so we did, although changing, at least for us, simply meant a shave and putting on aftershave and a jacket. For Declan, it meant the full works. Not only did he shave but he'd clearly washed his hair again and then blow-dried it; after that fairly magical transformation he'd dolled himself up in collar, tie and, even more to our surprise, a very tasty blue mohair suit. No wonder he'd had so much baggage.

Declan then led us to the one and only restaurant in Bantry which, once inside proved closer in character to a US Diner than anything else, but it was smart and extremely popular. The menu was a little lacking in sophistication but, if you liked anything that came from a pig, pretty extensive. There were pork chops, pork ribs, gammon steaks, pork sausages, ham and eggs, ham omelette, black pudding, white pudding, pork pies, pork & ham pies and pork meatballs. Or, if you were in a hurry or just wanted a take-away, ham sandwiches.

When it duly arrived (and I think all four of us opted for the Chef's Speciality, the mixed grill), it was extremely satisfying, if a little bland. Our only complaint was that the only refreshments available with it were tea or water. When we mentioned this to Declan he simply stared at us. "Sure, but 'tis only a restaurant; we'll be goin' to the pub afterwards."

And this we surely did. And not just to one, either. And each pub we managed to push our way into was packed to the bloody rafters with every kind of Irishman in varied stages of alcohol-induced merriment, from tipsy right through to being totally and utterly legless. After having elbowed our way to the bar in each of these establishments, Malcolm, Bobby and I began sneaking glances at one another. It was now close on 10.00 pm but nobody seemed to be making any move towards this dance that Declan had been so enthusiastic about. Furthermore, we hadn't spotted a single female all night. Not in the restaurant and neither in nor seated outside any of the pubs; all we'd come across were hordes of Irishmen all dressed up to the nines in their best suits, and all putting it away like prohibition would commence at midnight.

So, when Declan bellowed it was time to move on to the next pub, once we were in the street we sought to discover what the hell was going on. "Declan, it's almost ten o'clock – when are we going to this dance?"

"Not yet, me fine lads," he answered, "it's not closin' time yet."

"Yeah, but can't we just go to the dance now and have a few beers there?"

Declan stared at us. "I told yer – it's at the school. There'll be no alcoholic drinks there."

We stared at Declan in some astonishment although, even in our slightly befuddled state, what he said made sense. "OK," said Bobby, slowly, "but where are all the women?"

"At the school, of course," came the cheerful reply. "They'll have been there a-waitin' since about 7.30 pm."

"What? All by themselves?" I said. "Doing what?"

"And how in God's name would I know?" retorted Declan. "All I know is that they'll have arrived by bus from all around and they'll sit there, in the school, a-waitin' for us."

Malcolm, Bobby and I gazed at each other. After a pause, Bobby said, "All right, but when will we go to the school?"

Declan stared back at us, considering. Then, after a quick glance at his watch, he shrugged his shoulders and said, "Ah, what the hell, it's gone ten now. We might as well be goin' early and have a look over what's available tonight. But first we're goin' to have to get in some supplies." And with that, he headed back into the pub.

Supplies? What bloody supplies? Nevertheless, we followed our guide and mentor and pushed our way through to the bar, where Declan had managed to attract the attention of one of the perspiring, harried barmen. "Four small bottles of Paddy's an' twelve bottles of OBJs," he shouted, "all in the bags."

Paddy's? OBJs? Bags? Now what the fuck was happening? Our combined lack of comprehension was partially addressed when the barman ferried back to us a supply of four large brown paper bags, each containing a small bottle of Irish whiskey and four small bottles of beer. Having paid the barman, Declan shouted to us to each pick up a bag and to follow him outside. Once there, he stopped to face and educate us. "Yer not very bright tonight, me bhoys, are yer? Like I said, there'll be no alcohol at the school, and we've got to last out until midnight." He paused. "An' maybe beyond."

We stared at him, still not really understanding. "So what do we do with all this booze, then?" I enquired slowly.

Declan sighed, exasperated. "Well, we can't take it into the school," he explained patiently. "They'll be friskin' yer at the door; so we'll have to be a-hidin' it in the school grounds somewhere, an' come out for a quick one when we need it. But be careful not to be forgettin' where you hid it, nor leave it anywhere obvious so that some thievin' bastard can find it."

And that is exactly what we did. Having quickly sampled the contents of the bottles of "Oh Be Joyful" beers, we stashed our numerous bottles under a thickish bush not too close to the school entrance and, thus fortified, went over to join the dance.

Inside, the scene that greeted us had probably not changed that much in donkeys' years. The dance was held in the school hall at the far end of which was a platform. When we entered, to one side of the platform there was a small space occupied by a presumably local DJ, whose job was, seemingly, to entertain those present whilst the live band was setting up its gear for the gig. The left hand side of the hall was almost vacant, with but a handful of local lads who, apparently stricken with some kind of debilitating local paralysis, stood stock still in their best suits, gaping at the other side of the hall.

There, in serried ranks, were arrayed well over a hundred young women, and probably a good few more. The more brazen ones, those in the front rank, stared back at the as yet incomplete ranks of the opposite sex on the other side of the hall whilst those behind chattered quietly amongst themselves and, occasionally, having glanced at the would-be studs, giggled.

"Right," said Bobby, ever keen to display his machismo, "let's go, guys!"

Declan, however, tugged at his sleeve. "Not yet, me bhoy," he whispered fiercely, "are yer wantin' one of the ugly ones?"

At this professional warning, we took greater stock of the potential dancing partners facing us. Sure enough, although none of the women in the front rank were that ugly, the more attractive ones were certainly shielding themselves behind the front ranks. Bobby nodded slowly at this sage advice and whispered back, "So what d'we do?"

"Just hold yer horses awhile," muttered Declan. "We'll just talk amongst ourselves the while, so as not to look the village idjits like yer men down there and then, once the less discernin' of the bhoys arrive from the pub, we'll be much better placed to be mountin' an attack."

"How's that?" questioned Malcolm.

"Jaysus, Malcolm," said Declan, tartly, "have yer never been to a dance before?"

"Well, not like this."

"Ah, 'tis simple. When the drunker lads arrive, they'll neither know nor care what their partners will be lookin' like, so they get sent in, like shock troops. An' then, once five or six of the front row are out of the way, yer'll get a clear view of those behind, an' we'll be makin' our move."

And so it also proved. But if we'd hoped that, once we'd got our selected partners on the floor we'd be able to engage them in conversation and convince them what dashing and highly personable young men we were, we were sadly mistaken. Unlike in the UK, there were very definite protocols to be followed and, since we knew nothing whatsoever of these, each of Malcolm, Bobby and I initially found it all very confusing. To start with, if you asked a girl for a dance and she deemed you to be reasonably acceptable, she wouldn't say anything but just nodded her head and followed you to the dance floor. Then, there was none of the dancing with which we were most familiar. There was no jiving, no twist, no locomotion, no mashed potato, no hippy, hippy shake (not that I really knew what all of those were, anyway, nor how they truly differed from one another), nor any other form of "free" dancing. Instead, there were a few waltzes and foxtrots, but mostly what I took to be Irish jigs or whatever. What's more, actually talking to your partner whilst dancing was obviously strictly verboten, not that I had much time to do so as I was too occupied trying to work out where the hell my feet should go next, and generally failing.

Then, at just about the time you'd begin to think you might have cracked it, the band would stop and its leader, on the fiddle (no, I mean truly, not metaphorically) would both announce what the next dance would be, its derivation, plus various house-keeping tasks, such as where the band would be playing next week.

That was when I made my next faux pas. Whilst all this, to me, wholly uninteresting jabber was underway, I turned to my partner and tried to engage her in conversation. At this, she frowned at me accusingly and turned her head to better hear the band leader. Feeling summarily and ignominiously dismissed, I was turning away to creep back to my corner, when my partner caught my arm. "We've not finished dancin'," she stated, rather indignantly. Not finished? What had I missed? Was I stuck with this bird for the rest of the evening? None the less, I did as I was told but looked around me to see what was happening elsewhere. Malcolm, like me, had been caught unawares but Bobby, ever loathe to let go of a female once he felt he might have a captive audience, was engaged in animated conversation with his partner. Well, animated on his side.

Oh, well, in for a penny… so, I asked my partner what she meant, explaining I was from England and, over there, once the music stopped, dancers would part company. At this news, she regarded me with less hostility and explained that, at an Irish dance, you'd keep the same partner for three dances.

And that's what we did. At the end of my third effort to synchronize my less than praiseworthy movements with her's, she carefully let go of my hand and I escorted her back to the re-formed defensive ranks of females still holding sternly to the right hand side of the hall; but at least I received a parting smile from her, however condescending and wintry it might have been.

And that's how the few hours remaining for the dance progressed. At midnight, of course, we reached the start of the Sabbath and God forbid we should transgress upon that holy day with any merriment and enjoyment. Which he most certainly laid down, or at least, that's what the Roman Catholic Church in Ireland then believed and decreed. How many dances I had in that shortish period I cannot remember now, especially as it was broken by not infrequent visits outside the hall for a quick swig from our hidden treasures. Indeed, those external forays were far more memorable than the dances. As I emerged from the school, desperately trying to adjust my eyesight to the depth of night outside so I could locate the bush under which we'd hidden our illicit booty, I'd become aware that, all around me, others were involved in the same quest for their individual holy grails. There were never less than at least a dozen of them, and it was clear that a goodly percentage had forgotten exactly where they'd hidden their grog as they were blundering about, clearly the worse for wear. Amid mumbled curses and groans, the seekers were looking in, under and around bushes, behind and even up trees, in gutters and drains and just about anywhere else that anyone with any degree of initiative and desire to ensure the safety of their cache might have hidden it. Furthermore, their efforts were not improved by the obstacles placed in their paths by the more successful of their fellow seekers who, having been triumphantly re-united with their booze, proceeded to enjoy their contents by sitting on the floor with their backs to trees and walls, from which position they shouted wholly inappropriate and sometimes physically impossible advice to their increasing frantic fellow treasure hunters. In addition, there were one or two happy souls whose interest in returning to the dance had clearly ebbed away, as indeed, had their consciousness, leaving their somnolent bodies sprawled in the grass to trip up the incautious or incapable.

When the bell tolled at midnight to end the dance, wielded energetically and imperiously by a stern-faced senior staff member of the school, it did indeed toll for most of us, male and female. The vast majority of the dancers trooped out of the school to the various waiting buses, the girls chattering animatedly amongst themselves and frequently giggling at the glum and disappointed visages of the would-be Romeos who either morosely boarded the buses or who set off on the walk home.

Malcolm and I had failed to persuade any of the local beauties to extend their stay in Bantry as indeed, much to our surprise, had Declan. He, however, passed off such lack of success by airily stating that none of the girls present that night really matched up to his ideal in any event, an assurance that Malcolm and I took with carefully adopted blank expressions. Bobby, on the other hand, seemed to have come up trumps as not only did he leave the school hall still with his partner but they were actually holding hands. So, acting in accordance with unwritten rules, we nonchalantly ignored Bobby, despite his irritating wink and the swagger with which he wandered off into the night.

Next morning, I struggled up at about 9.30 am and wandered down to the tiny room in which breakfast was served. Not only was Malcolm ahead of me but so was Bobby, looking distinctly the worse for wear, his clothes muddy and creased. "Blimey, Bobby," I said to him, "I didn't expect you to be up from bed so early. Haven't you changed since last night?"

Malcolm said nothing but grinned mischievously. Bobby raised his head and, having semi-snarled at Malcolm soundlessly, sullenly responded "I haven't been to bed," and thereafter fell silent.

"Oh, right," I said, "you obviously got on well, then."

"No, I fucking didn't," came the sharp reply.

"How come?" asked Malcolm who, like me, was genuinely curious.

"Well, as she lived in a small house on the other side of Bantry Bay, all by itself, and there was no bus available, we had to walk."

"So how did she get in for the dance?"

"Some friends of her parents were coming into Bantry early in the evening and gave her a lift in their car. But they went back home at about 10.00 pm."

"So how far was it, back to her house?"

"I don't fucking know," Bobby retorted with some exasperation.

"Why?" I queried. "What happened?"

"We never got there – to her place!" Bobby snarled. "We set off OK but, after we'd been gone about half an hour, I asked her how much further it was and all she said was 'It's just a step aroun' the next corner.'"

"So?" I asked.

"Well, we just kept on fucking walking, God knows how far. And by this time we were down to pretty much a dirt road, without any lighting. And then it started fucking raining."

"So then what?" queried Malcolm, with increasing interest?

"She was all right; she had a clear plastic poncho in her handbag. But I had nothing and got absolutely bloody soaked. Not only that but, in the fucking dark I kept wandering off the road and fell down twice – look at my clothes; I'm nearly covered in mud!" And so he was, too. Malcolm and I smiled even more; this was getting better and better.

"So how did it all finish?" I asked.

"After we'd been walking up that sodding road for just over two hours, I asked her again how much bloody further it was. And so help me she simply said again, 'Oh, just a step aroun' the next corner'. And when I said, 'But we've been around at least three corners since I last asked you that', she had the fucking nerve to say, 'Ah, those weren't corners – they were just bends in the road.'"

Internally, Malcolm and I hugged ourselves with glee; better and better still. "And then what happened?"

"What d'you fucking think?" Bobby replied with some irritation. "I told her I wasn't going any further – enough was enough. So we shook hands and I started back to Bantry."

"Well, that wasn't very gentlemanly," I observed. "That poor girl must have had all her illusions about English gentlemen totally shattered; wouldn't you say, Malcolm?"

"Absolutely disgraceful behaviour," confirmed Malcolm. "You or I wouldn't have done that would we, Carruthers?"

"Oh, fuck off," came Bobby's snarled response.

"Then you didn't manage to… you know?" enquired Malcolm delicately.

"You know what?" demanded Bobby aggressively.

"You know – get your leg, you know, get your leg over?" continued Malcolm.

"Get my leg over?" echoed Bobby irascibly. "I didn't even get a snog, let alone a fucking shag."

We all sat there contemplating for a few moments; Malcolm and I in disguised silent mirth (well, almost disguised) and Bobby in sullen self-pity at the unfairness of it all. "What time did you get back then?" I asked Bobby, more to break the silence than because I had any real interest.

"About twenty minutes ago," came the very short reply.

We sat there without speaking for a few moments more, Malcolm and I glancing at one another and trying to keep our faces straight. Then a thought struck Malcolm. "Wait a sec," he mused aloud. "If you left us at just after midnight and then walked with your Irish rose for about two hours, how come it took you nearly seven hours to get back?"

"Because not only did it piss down with rain but, after I took shelter in an abandoned stone croft for a while, when I came out I couldn't find the road at first. Then, when I did, I couldn't remember, in the dark, which was the way back to Bantry until a farmer came along in a horse and trap at about 7.30 am. Luckily, he was coming into Bantry and gave me a lift."

After that, whenever Bobby subsequently became boastful about his exploits with the opposite sex, Malcolm and I only had to inject the words 'Bantry' or 'Ireland' into the conversation and Bobby would come to a stuttering halt. Irish eyes might have been smiling after that dance but Bobby's certainly weren't.

DEATH SHALL HAVE NO DOMINION

As I've stated elsewhere, back in the 1960s, money was a great deal scarcer and the possession of personal transportation a great deal more limited. Furthermore, Rugby Union was even more of a minority sport than it is now and clubs, at least away from the larger cities and towns, were not often that geographically close to one another. Certainly, not where I lived, on the edge of Southend, out on the Essex coast. Apart from the town's elder and premier club, Southend RFC, with whom we enjoyed a wonderfully sporting but sometimes heavy-handed and less than totally chivalrous rivalry, our next nearest opponents were at Chelmsford. Otherwise, we had to travel to places like Barking, on the periphery of London, or into London itself. Even so, the lack of opposition of approximate equality meant that we also had to accept fixtures against clubs that lay even further afield, such as Colchester and Ipswich, plus clubs in Kent. Away trips to the last group were regarded as almost a tour abroad; this was before the construction of the Dartford Tunnel and we'd leave our own clubhouse before noon and often not return until nearly midnight. Crossing the Thames at Tilbury was thus much akin to going overseas and the populace found there was therefore initially treated with the kind of trepidation and suspicion afforded most foreigners. Quite right and very wise, too.

In consequence, given that the smaller rugby clubs generally lived fairly hand-to-mouth, funds were religiously guarded and, for their treasurers, the much preferred means by which to transport teams to away matches was in cars belonging to the players involved. It therefore stood to reason that the fewer the number of vehicles required, the less would be claimed as expenses, overall. Indeed, when I first started playing senior rugby, most clubs (and certainly my own) would not even reimburse travelling expenses such as these – just before you returned home, late on the Saturday evening, tired and cramped in the back of a team-mate's vehicle, the hat would be passed around for contributions to the cost of fuel incurred by the driver – petrol money.

Thus owning a large vehicle could often cement your place in a team that, had you not owned it, might well have been considered beyond your actual playing aspirations. Considering now how few families do not own cars, with some having up to three or more if two or three adult children are still living at home, it was truly a different world then, just fifty or so years ago. In addition, very few women then owned or even drove cars; it was almost entirely a male privilege. And very few men, at least in my rugby club, owned new cars, apart from one or two flash buggers.

Suddenly turning up with a large vehicle was therefore an event of note as it placed you in the patrician class; well, as near as we ever came to coming in contact with one such. In consequence, such a feat of forthcoming ownership of a vehicle was not one that you generally kept to yourself. It was something to be carefully tossed into a casual discussion some time ahead of the vehicle's arrival so as to enjoy to the maximum the congratulations of your friends and, better still, the hopefully poorly disguised demonstrations of envy of others.

One such announcement was made one Thursday evening when we had repaired to our club for a re-hydrating session after pre-season training in mid-August. The news was put about by not Ron, the allegedly newly socially uplifted individual concerned, a schoolmaster at our local high school, but by one of his colleagues there, Doug. Now we all know that there is every chance that stories that get passed around gain much in their repeated telling, and our first reaction to Doug's information was to be more than a little incredulous, especially as he had long been known to, how shall I put it? Gild the lily more often than not?

"Truly, I kid you not," protested Doug to our knowing looks and poorly hidden disbelief, "that's what has happened."

One or two late comers to the bar had not heard the original proclamation, so Doug was forced to make it all over again. Since this made him increasingly the centre of attraction, he did this willingly and with much relish. "Ron received a letter, on Monday, I think he said, from a firm of lawyers up in York. It was one of those letters that you see portrayed in films where the hero is asked to contact the lawyers because they had information that would be to his advantage."

Doug really had our attention now and, realising it, he masterfully delayed his story by pausing for a pull at his glass. "Go on, Doug, don't piss about, what happened?" he was asked.

"Well, Ron rang these lawyers and found that his great uncle had died and left him a bequest in his will."

"Yeah, what?"

"Well, you're not going to believe this," continued Doug.

"What? What did he leave Ron?"

"A roller."

"A roller?" We paused to consider this. "A roller? D'you mean a Rolls Royce?"

Pleased with the semi-incredulous manner in which we'd received his news, Doug nodded. "Yeah. A real, honest-to-goodness Rolls Royce."

We looked at one another. Could this be true? Really and truly? "G'wan," someone snorted dismissively. "More like a pair of bloody roller skates."

"No, Ron assures me it's true," responded Doug.

At this, we all fell silent for the moment, digesting the thought of Ron driving around in a roller. Blimey, perhaps he'd drive up to the school in it – how would the Boot, the school's much revered and feared headmaster, take that? "So when is Ron going to get his hands on this roller?" queried another in our group.

Doug scratched his head. "Ah, that's a bit of a problem as Ron doesn't drive, and the bloody thing's up in York."

"So what's Ron going to do? How's he going to get it down here? Or is he simply going to sell it?"

At this rather less magical but much more practical and realistic idea was grasped, most of us nodded; if Ron didn't even drive then selling the car certainly made much more sense. Doug quickly rekindled our interest, however. "Ron hasn't made up his mind yet but I think he's promised to let the lawyer know tomorrow morning. Problem is, the Boot will never let him have time off to go up there and collect it during the week, and hiring someone to drive it down here will be pretty expensive, even before you consider just the cost of the petrol."

There being no further information to be gleaned from Doug, we all gave our attention to more immediate and mundane matters, such as whose was the next round, so thoughts of Ron's good fortune were shelved for the time being.

Shortly afterwards that evening and apropos of exactly nothing, Sid, our hooker, put the arm on me.

Sid had been the year above me at school and, shortly after leaving, had achieved one of his major ambitions in life; he was accepted into the RAF. Whilst this had meant that he disappeared off into the blue yonder for a few years, being stationed in various distant locations such as Germany, Cyprus and Singapore, he had recently reappeared after being posted to an aerodrome in Cambridge somewhere. Just after we had all mulled over the prospect of Ron becoming a car owner, and presumably prompted by such news, Sid grabbed me for a moment and asked if I could do him a big favour.

"Sure, Sid," I said, rather too casually, "What d'you want?"

"Well, I've just bought a car," he said, "a Ford Anglia."

I smiled at him with unthinking pleasure. "Excellent, Sid. That'll make it much easier for you to get here each weekend."

"Exactly," he confirmed, "but I have a small problem."

"What's that Sid?"

"Like Ron, I can't drive; I don't have a license yet."

I regarded Sid with some surprise but not yet any suspicion. "So what's the favour you want of me?"

"Well, could you drive me back to the base on Saturday? I'll stand you lunch in the Mess and pay for your train fare back here; so what d'you reckon?"

I glanced at Sid again and thought about his request. I hadn't got anything planned for the Saturday and a pleasant drive up to Cambridgeshire before lunch and a train journey home, all at Sid's expense, seemed a more than agreeable idea. "Yeah; sure, Sid. No problem."

He looked at me earnestly for a second then asked, "Are you really sure? Only it's extremely important I report there with my car by no later than midday Saturday."

Still I saw no storm warnings, even though I felt the slight rustling of a breeze from somewhere. "No, that's fine, Sid – sounds like a good day out."

"So I can wholly rely on you, can I?"

The wind was picking up now but Sid being an officer and maybe even a gentleman, I knew he'd be punctilious about reporting back to his base on time. "Don't be such a silly sod, Sid – of course I'll do it. I've just said so, haven't I?"

Sid gave a perceptible sigh of relief and smiled at me. "Great," he said, "you've solved a real problem for me."

"Like I said, Sid, no problem." Then, thinking ahead, I asked, "What time d'you want me to pick you up on Saturday morning? About 10.00? Or is that a little too early?"

"Oh, no," replied Sid, smiling secretly, "It'll need to be much earlier than that."

The wind was nearly at gale force now and I began to feel its existence. "Much earlier? How much earlier?"

"Probably around 5.00; certainly no later than that."

I stared at Sid in amazement, now fully aware of the storm cones. "No later than 5.00? On a Saturday morning? For fuck's sake, why? It's no more than a couple of hours drive to Cambridge."

"Oh, didn't I tell you? I've been posted up north, to Linton-on-Ouse – I've got to report for duty there at midday on Saturday."

Linton-on-Ouse? Where the fuck was Linton-on-Ouse? Searching my memory produced absolutely nothing but, wherever it was, it sounded wet and a long way away. "Where's Linton-on-Ouse, for Christ's sake, Sid? How far north? It's not in Scotland, is it?" I finished, with mounting concern.

He grinned at me, a little mischievously. "Just past York," he informed me.

"Just past York?" I responded. "But that's bloody miles!"

Sid nodded his head in agreement. "Yeah – about 240 miles, according to the map."

"You cunning little bastard!" I accused him after a pause. "You bloody well conned me!" He smiled back, smugly – I had to laugh. "You're not as stupid as you look!"

"Which, obviously, is more than I can say for you. Anyway, I truly am grateful" Sid replied. "Come on, I'll buy you a drink."

It was such a good story that I had tell the others still at the bar how Sid had manoeuvred me into driving him to his new base on Saturday morning. Whilst most grinned at Sid's chicanery, Doug looked thoughtful. "Just past York you say?" he enquired. "You wouldn't be interested in taking Ron with you and, after you've dropped off Sid, going into York and picking up his roller before driving it and Ron back here, would you?"

I thought about it quickly. Why not? Especially as I'd get the opportunity to drive a roller all the way from York back to Southend. "Yeah," I nodded, "why not? You don't have any objections do you, Sid? There'll be enough room in the Anglia, won't there? Even with all your kit?"

Sid not only couldn't think of any impediment, he could also see the financial advantage he'd get from not having to pay my train fare back from Yorkshire to Southend. And so, Doug having immediately phoned Ron to put the proposal to him, it was all agreed. At least once Ron had contacted the lawyers and got them to agree to meeting him at midday on Saturday to complete all the paperwork and hand over his great-uncle's Rolls Royce.

Saturday morning, initially driving my own car, I first picked up Ron, at the unearthly hour of 4.30 a.m., just before dawn had begun to lighten the eastern horizon, and we grumpily drove round to Sid's parent's house. There, thankfully, Sid and his car were already prepared and waiting for us so Ron and I clambered into the Anglia and set off to darkest Yorkshire.

The journey up to York was fairly uneventful, except for Sid being concerned that if I went up above sixty, the new love of his life would suffer irreparable damage before he'd even had the chance to lovingly get to know her, whilst Ron regularly urged me to crack on as fast as possible so as to get to York before the lawyer concerned decided he'd already put himself out far more than was called for and went home. Given the almost universal disdain of all the lawyers I'd met for the desires of their clients as compared to their own, I was very much of the same mind as Ron. In consequence, I kept pushing the Anglia as fast as I could, all the while assuring Sid that there was nothing better for a car than giving it a good, hard, long run. For some reason, my confident claims seemed to reassure him less and less, especially after a slight, initially almost indiscernible knocking noise first started to sound about fifty miles short of York and gradually, but perceptibly, became more noticeable, particularly to Sid.

We stopped for a quick breakfast and a piss at a roadside café on the A1 at about 8.00 am but still made it to the lawyers' premises in York just after 11.00. There, as we'd agreed in advance, we dropped Ron to complete all whatever legal formalities would be required and then I drove Sid onto the RAF base at Linton-on-Ouse. Sadly, I had agreed with Ron that I'd have to pass on Sid's offer of lunch in the Mess since, like Ron; I wanted to get back to Southend fairly early that evening. Even so, Sid had to take me to the Mess, simply to both introduce himself and to persuade a fellow officer to drive me back into York to meet up with Ron again. However, with all the "hail-fellow-well-met" greetings that Sid had to get through, it was only at about 12.30 pm that I escaped and was driven back to York by a very affable new playmate of Sid's.

Turning the corner to the street where we'd dropped him off earlier, I saw Ron sitting on the step of the lawyers' offices holding both a superb, black silk top hat and a large, buff envelope in his hands. To my surprise, he didn't look the happy bunny I'd expected; shit, had he been unable to complete the documentation and take possession of the roller? If so, how the hell were we going to get home?

I stepped out of my lift to greet Ron as he, seeing it was me, clambered to his feet. Before I could ask my driver if he could wait a second, lest we needed a lift to York's railway station, he bid me a cheery goodbye and sped off, presumably to lunch. Plan B having gone out of the window before it could even be articulated, I turned to Ron. "What's up? You don't look too happy, Ron. Wouldn't the lawyer let you have the Rolls?"

Ron gazed at me expressionlessly. "No," he said, "I've got the Rolls; it's just down here in the courtyard at the back."

So saying, he led me down a passageway that led to a smallish yard. There, he turned and gestured to the vehicle standing there. Well, it was big, it was black and shiny and it was undeniably a Rolls Royce. And, in its way, it was utterly compelling and extremely beautiful.

Problem was, it was a hearse, and not the newest one I'd ever seen either.

I turned to Ron who stood there with a carefully non-committal look on his face. "So what are we going to do now?" I asked. "D'you still want to take it back home?"

Ron looked back at me and shrugged. "What else can we do? I'd planned on selling it once we got back down south in any event, since the market for a roller is better down there anyway. And in discussions with the lawyer today he told me he'd already made a few enquiries up here but found absolutely no interest for it."

We both stood and stared at the gleaming, opulent vehicle that was parked in front of us with such innate elegance. "How long will it take us to get home in this thing?" I asked. "What sort of speed can it do? Or was it built to just poodle around in a very low gear all the way to the crematorium?"

"I haven't the faintest idea," said Ron. "Oh well, we might as well get in and see how we go," and tossed me the keys.

We carefully opened the two front doors and gingerly stepped inside. I have to say that, as bizarre the circumstances, it really was the most magnificently impressive vehicle I'd ever been in. We sat there in silence for a few minutes, reverentially taking in all the details of the interior which now, sadly, have become misty and more than a little obscure with the passage of time. The seats, I do remember, were of real and thick leather and had clearly been lovingly kept in wonderful good order. The woodwork of the dashboard was magnificent; it far outshone the dining-room table my mother had inherited with such pride from her mother. Thus, everything up front was all that you could have expected from a first entry into a Rolls Royce; it was only when you looked over your shoulder that the illusion of being a plutocrat shivered.

I can't believe that there's anyone that cannot readily visualise the appearance of a hearse, not just the outside but also the interior, so I won't bother to detail what was behind us. I'll just say that it had, like the rest of the vehicle, been beautifully constructed from the highest quality materials, although the central plinth had clearly seen a fair degree of use. After a second or two's silent observation, Ron and I glanced at each other and turned back to more pragmatic matters.

Firstly, I gingerly inserted the ignition keys and turned on the engine. Except it didn't. Or I didn't think it had. Just to be sure, I pressed the accelerator and, after a slight delay, I became aware of a faint murmur somewhere. I glanced at Ron but he was more interested in the dials on the dashboard, most especially that showing how much fuel was in the tank. To his manifest distress, the needle was pressed firmly and irrevocably against the zero. "Bastards!" he snarled. "That bloody lawyer's left me with nothing in the tank! How the hell are we even going to get to the nearest petrol station, let alone back to Southend?"

"How the fuck should I know?" I replied, not immediately realising Ron's query was more rhetorical than personal.

"Well, we'd better find out, and fast!" stated Ron, climbing out of the roller. "And turn that bloody engine off, now!"

We therefore spent almost twenty minutes accosting passing pedestrians before we found one who was even vaguely helpful, but he not only knew of a petrol station reasonably close at hand but also agreed to ride with us to ensure we found it. There, we put over twenty gallons into the tank whilst Ron's eyes got wider and wider and his eyebrows climbed higher and higher as, with petrol costing four shillings and sixpence a gallon (22.5p in today's money) he mentally kept track of the serious damage being wreaked on his wallet. Finally, the attendant finished filling the tank and Ron despondently and begrudgingly handed over just in excess of five pounds. Christ, I thought, that's almost enough to buy a barrel of beer. I calculated quickly; well, getting on for fifty pints of bitter.

We climbed silently into the Rolls; Ron in depressed gloom and me in silent commiseration at his pain. And thus our journey started. It was all suitably solemn and stately to start with as I'd never been in York before and also was more than a little fearful of poorly handling a car which was about twice as big as anything I'd ever driven previously. If I damaged the roller somehow I'd never forgive myself and Ron wouldn't have been too ecstatic, either. Somehow, despite neither of us having had the foresight to bring a map of York with us, we managed to get out of the city, and on its south side as well. Given that I wanted to concentrate on driving the roller without committing any errors, and not just punishable ones, I was not unhappy that Ron decided to busy himself with going through the various papers he'd extracted from the buff envelope he'd presumably been given by the lawyer. "It's a Phantom II," he announced, "3340 cc, 25/30 hp, first registered on 31 October 1936."

"Halloween? Is that a good or a bad omen?" I asked.

"Highly suitable for its purpose, anyway," responded Ron gloomily.

He continued going through all his papers whilst I managed, by some minor miracle, to find our way via the A64, through Tadcaster, to the A1. Now, in those days, the A1 was not the A1 as we know it now, with much of its length having been upgraded to motorway standards. Motorway standards? What the hell were they? Yes, there were some decent stretches of dual carriageways but a significant amount of the A1 was still only a single carriageway, albeit of sufficient width to accommodate three cars. However, the width of lorries made it ill-advisable to overtake one when another was coming in the opposite direction. Thankfully, this being a Saturday, there were a lot fewer lorries on the road than normal. Even so, it was therefore not until we came to the first stretch of dual carriageway that I felt bold enough to put my foot down to try and discover (as I had been hankering to do all along) what this Rolls Royce could do.

Initially, the response was a little disappointing. Yes, the roller picked up speed, but not with the kind of oomph that I thought would be delivered by what, in those days, was such a bloody enormous engine. But then I realised the acceleration, although accompanied by hardly any extra sound from the engine, was smoothly continuous. Soon, we were gliding serenely along at nearly 60 mph but, at that point, the vehicle clearly decided that to go any faster would be both distasteful and wholly out of keeping and loftily refused to go any faster. Just as well as it happened. Having finished going through all his documents, Ron had glanced up and, seeing we were now moving considerably faster, glanced at the speedometer to presumably see at exactly what speed we were now travelling. However, his attention was then attracted to the dial showing how full our petrol tank was.

"Jesus fucking Christ," he shouted, "have you seen how much petrol we've already consumed?"

In fact, I hadn't, and when I now checked I was as equally appalled as Ron was to see that the needle on the dial was already quivering between half and two-thirds full. "Shit," I remarked and, after glancing at the milometer reading, "and we've only covered just over 60 miles!"

Ron stared at the gauge with fascinated horror. "But that means," he started, completing some rapid mental arithmetic, "that we're getting, er, less than 12 mpg! A lot less, in fact."

I did my own similar calculations and then extrapolated them further. "At that rate of consumption, we're going to need nearly fifty gallons to get this thing home."

Ron turned to me, a doomsday look on his face. "But I've only got just over another ten pounds on me." He paused whilst he considered the situation; and remember, there were no credit cards or cash machines dotted around the place in those days. "How much have you got on you?"

I winced in some embarrassment. Expecting a free day out, I had not bothered to replenish my wallet to any great extent on Friday. "Only about nine or ten quid," I confessed.

Ron took in this less than wholly encouraging news fairly well, all things considered. He considered our options swiftly and then stated, "OK; with a bit of luck we should make it, but we'll have to drop our speed a lot."

I nodded as this made good sense, even though it would materially lengthen the time of our journey. And that's what we did, bringing the Rolls down to a much more sedate forty miles an hour, watching rather forlornly as numerous vehicles, often forced to queue in processions behind us until the road widened, roared past us with irritated toots on the horns and withering looks of disdain.

Finally, we drove up outside the rugby club, with less than twenty minutes to spare before closing time, and sped inside for critically needed refreshment and rehydration. Inside, the rapturous applause with which we were greeted by the small band of loyal and battle-hardened drinkers still left standing that Saturday night went a long way towards compensating for our nerve-ridden drive home, watching the fuel gauge almost more than the road ahead as it moved inexorably down towards our being stranded out in the boondocks in the pitch dark, penniless.

Apparently, we'd missed a wonderful evening as the related cricket club's second team, hosting mostly idle rugby club members, had enjoyed a famous win over the third team of the most powerful cricket club in the area; one whose coach was Trevor Bailey, the England all-rounder. Not only that, but one of the rugby players, opening the batting in the absence of any cricket club member of any note in the team, had scored a maiden century. Well, that of course meant that seemingly endless jugs of beer had to be purchased by that worthy until, at about 9.00 pm, he slid, mindlessly smiling, into deep and contented, if fund-less unconsciousness. Indeed, he was still present, stretched out on the bench to which he'd been lovingly carried by his friends and hangers-on, many of whom appeared to be very close to joining him.

Of course, once Ron and I had been bought beers of our own and been taken on a guided tour of the unconscious leviathan, there rapidly grew a clamour to view the roller, the transport of princes and kings, ownership of which had always been considered a total impossibility to mere mortals such as we. This could not be done immediately as Ron and I needed to regale our listeners with the tale of derring-do that had occurred.

Finally, at just after 11.00 pm, Ron and I led a crowd of about eight weaving, owl-faced spectators, all clutching desperately at their half-filled beer glasses to steady themselves, out to inspect the roller. They all expressed suitably admiring comments, even though some of them might not have been that capable of actually seeing the vehicle. One newly self-appointed devotee was so impressed with the vehicle that he elegantly draped himself over the bonnet and, overcome with emotion, proceeded to fall asleep there. The remainder of our group ignored him and, having admiringly wandered around the roller, demanded to look inside and, most particularly, at the rear area.

Having peered soundlessly through the open rear of the vehicle for a few minutes, it was agreed, by unspoken mutual consent, that we'd been away from the bar for far too long and, almost as one, we turned and shuffled back on a gently meandering course to the clubhouse. After less than an hour after closing time, and with the lights mostly extinguished to save on unnecessary electricity costs, the random debates that had occurred gradually became focussed on a proposal from Doug, Ron's colleague at the local high school. Doug felt that it would somehow be less than appropriate for the Rolls Royce to celebrate its new ownership so mundanely; instead, we should take it on a practice run to exercise its design capabilities.

We considered this thought with careful dignity, although I suspect that not all of those present had a clue of what Doug was talking about. "But where?" asked Ron, ultimately, whilst others nodded sagaciously.

Doug thought for a moment. "How about up and down Southend High Street?" he suggested. "We could start at Victoria Circus and finish at the top of Pier Hill."

"Why?" asked Ron, after a few seconds.

"Why not?" retorted Doug.

Being unable to come up with any logical answer, Ron nodded and shrugged his shoulders in passive agreement. Ron and I then left the barman to close up the bar and the clubhouse whilst our remaining four co-conspirators unsteadily wandered out to the roller.

Initially, there was a short period of confusion when John came to realise it was not that far off midnight. "Christ," he remarked, "is that really the time? I'll have to go home; if I don't my wife will kill me."

Jimmy shrugged his shoulders. "Why worry? You'll be in the ideal place for that, here in the hearse."

John blinked a couple of times before acknowledging Jimmy's unassailable logic and clambered gingerly into the back of the roller, where Jimmy and Doug made him lie down on the plinth, face upwards and arms crossed on his chest. "Preparing for Judgment Day," Jimmy explained.

With Ron and I up front and John the body with the three mourners in the back, we drove slowly from Leigh to Southend, eliciting a number of curious stares from the occupants of the few cars that passed us. Just before we arrived in Southend, however, John began complaining of feeling ill. Doug, Jimmy and Grumpy did their best to reassure John it was nothing to be concerned about. "Certainly," assured Doug, "it's nothing fatal." Then, as a fresh thought took him, Doug came up with a suggested remedy he was certain would be highly efficacious. "I know just the thing to make you feel better," he pronounced firmly, "dahlias!"

There was a longish silence whilst the rest of us thought about this. Dahlias? Weren't they bloody flowers? What the fuck was Doug on about? Sensing our disbelief, Doug loftily elucidated. "I've no doubt the rest of you ignorant sods are not aware of this but dahlias were originally introduced to this country as a medicinal herb."

The rest of us slipped surreptitious glances at another. Was Doug taking the piss or something? "Yeah?" said Jimmy, less than convinced. "What d'you do? Boil the flowers, or something?"

"No, no," said Doug sharply, "don't you daft buggers know anything? It's not the heads but the bulbs that are ingested."

"What, like an onion?" asked Grumpy, scratching his head.

"Well, more or less," answered Doug, now on less sure ground.

"So, how d'you eat it?" queried Ron. "D'you cook it or eat it raw?"

"Oh, either way," declared Doug.

"Well, it doesn't matter if you stick it up your arse," commented Jimmy, "where the fuck are we going to find dahlia bulbs at this time of night?"

At this point, John returned briefly to the land of the living. "I think I'm going to be sick," he remarked weakly.

"What!" shouted Ron, "No, you fucking don't! Not in my hearse!" He then turned to me. "Quick! Pull over!"

"No, no!" countermanded Doug. "Drive on to Victoria Circus! They've planted an entire display there, of dahlias and begonias. Quick, don't fart about!"

Reacting as swiftly as I could to the last instructions my brain had received, we shot forward to Victoria Circus. Sure enough, planted right across this large floral roundabout were swathes of colourful blooms. "That's it," shouted Doug, "stop just here! These are all dahlias! At least, I think so," he added with less conviction.

"So now what?" asked Grumpy.

"Dig up some dahlias of course, piss-head!" snapped Doug.

And so we did. With some will and energy, but not a great deal of skill. Soon, we had a collection of some twenty or more flowers with their bulbs which were ferried to John, now sitting, very pale-faced, on the open rear of the roller. He looked at the selection being offered him and, although the flower-heads were unarguably resplendent, it was the bulbs that were shoved under his nose, most of them still carrying spattering of the earth from which they'd been so unceremoniously yanked.

John stared at these highly unappetising offerings and, in front of our very eyes, turned a delicate shade of light green. Slightly miffed at this lack of appreciation of his medical knowledge, Doug quickly dusted off the earth attached to one of the bulbs he'd offered John and backed up his prescription with not untypical bravado. "John, John," he cajoled that unfortunate, "it really will make you feel much better. Look!" And so saying, he selected the largest bulb in his clutch and took a large bite out of it.

The rest of us stared at him in amazed fascination. Had Doug lost his marbles? "Mmm," he observed, in between chews, "not bad. Not bad at all," and he bit another large chunk from the bulb. Saving John, who continued to observe the world in a miserable silence, the rest of us gawped at both Doug and one another. Then Jimmy, as if slightly mesmerised by Doug's behaviour, also took a bite at a bulb, as did both Grumpy and Ron after a hesitant pause.

"D'you know," opined Doug, "these are really quite tasty – bit sharp, but I've certainly had worse."

Jimmy, having chewed slowly and with some suspicion on a bulb of his own, gradually nodded his head in apparent agreement. "You're right. They've a flavour all their own and it, well, it sort of grows on you."

"That's true," agreed Doug, "that's very true. In fact, I'm going to try some more," and he moved back to the town's prized flower beds, followed soon after by Jimmy.

Grumpy and Ron, however, were far less taken with dahlias au naturel and, the two gourmands having departed, carefully spat out the chewed remains of their own samples, with a considerable shaking of heads. This action was the last straw for John who'd been valiantly trying to hold down the increasingly rebellious contents of his stomach. Leaning forward, he regurgitated a considerable volume of liquid and partially digested edibles onto the floor with some force.

We should have expected it; after all, there had been enough warning signs. But it was late, we'd had a long, tiring and emotionally charged day, and our colleagues' reactions had also been pretty well deadened by alcohol. In consequence, instead of stepping back when John emptied his insides, we simply stood there in static horror. Having such a high liquid content, the splash effect was incredibly extreme. Or not, depending where you were standing. Being much to the fore, Grumpy caught by far the highest proportion, which liberally covered his trousers from the knees down. It's difficult to articulate exactly the sound that Grumpy made as it was more animal than human, but it was not unknown for Grumpy to over-react. Anyway, after his first guttural reaction, Grumpy was less than sympathetic to poor John. "You bastard," he shouted, "look what you've fucking done!"

It was, I have to admit, a little distasteful, but Grumpy was wearing some old tan cords and, to my eyes, it really didn't show up that badly; well, not in that light anyway. More disastrous, and taken deeply to his heart, was the desolation caused to Grumpy's pride and joy, his sand-coloured, suede Jesus boots. "You absolute cunt!" he bellowed, "you've totally fucked my boots!"

It took a few minutes after that to bring matters back to an equilibrium. Ron, after the first shock of John's assault on Grumpy's sartorial elegance, was not that fazed, especially as he'd only been on the periphery of the splash-zone. In addition, he was highly relieved that John's ejection had not incurred inside the hearse. Grumpy, however, remained highly incensed at having become, as he mysteriously claimed, a sacrificial lamb, and insisted, since he lived not too far away, on storming off home. Thus he was absent for the final twist to the story of the day's events.

Meanwhile, both Doug and Jimmy were off in a world of their own. Not only had they failed to register the contretemps between John and Grumpy but they had somehow managed to create a competition between themselves to see who could eat the most dahlia bulbs. As a result, whilst Ron was keeping a very wary eye on John lest he suddenly took it upon himself to let fly with another violent internal disgorgement, I was sent out to try and bring our two waifs and strays back to the hearse. Although it was past midnight by now, it was not difficult to find them. Not only was the area brightly lit with streetlamps all around the roundabout, but they had left a swathe of desolation right across it, with discarded and half-eaten bulbs strewed to left and right. Indeed, when I finally caught up with them, nearly on the far side of the roundabout, they were engaged in what could only be described a slow-motion argument, with carefully enunciated and simultaneous accusations and rejections being accompanied by ill-directed one-fingered pokes in each other's chests.

From what I could gather, Doug was claiming he'd eaten over twenty dahlia bulbs, which Jimmy was disputing vociferously on the grounds that Doug had only taken a bite, and sometimes hardly even a nibble out of each. By comparison, Jimmy pointed out that he'd conscientiously consumed thirteen dahlia bulbs in their entirety, including some of the stalks and flowers.

Still maintaining and expanding the justifications for their separate claims, we all slowly wended our way across the top of the roundabout towards the roller and, when Doug caught sight of it again, he suddenly recalled the original reason why we'd come into Southend. "Right," he proclaimed, "let's drive down the High Street to Pier Hill. Tell you what, I'll lie down on the plinth to make it look more realistic" and, without more ado, Doug climbed into the back of the hearse and positioned himself, face up, on the plinth in the back. Ron watched him with some suspicion at first but then, having installed John, now becoming more and more compos mentis, next to me up front, decided our process up and down Southend High Street needed to be properly institutionalised. He therefore took out the black top hat that the lawyers had handed him and, having manoeuvred himself round to the front of the vehicle, gave me a grave nod and began striding slowly and imperiously in front of me down Southend High Street.

We had proceeded in this fashion to almost Southend Central Railway Station, Ron solemnly slow marching about five paces ahead of me and with Doug lying in statuesque isolation in the back, when a blue, flashing light in my mirrors signalled that we were not alone. Slowly, cautiously and with a degree of puzzlement, a police car overtook us with the two officers inside peering at our little procession. They then signalled for us to pull over and pulled ahead of us before gently coming to a halt next to the curb. Aided by Ron's careful and elaborate hand signals, I pulled the roller over to the kerb a few cards behind the patrol vehicle and sat there, awaiting the passage of events.

The two officers climbed out of their car and, putting on their peaked caps, walked back to where Ron, magnificently resplendent in his shiny black topper, stood awaiting them in a wonderfully adopted pose of casual superiority. "Excuse me, sir," said one officer, "but what exactly are you doing?"

Ron looked down his nose with marvellous disdain and responded that we were observing the final rites of one of our dearest friends, now newly departed. The two officers glanced at each other with expressions that clearly indicated that they'd come across a Saturday night nutcase and asked Ron, with amazingly apparent courtesy, who might that be. Ron played it to the full, to the end. "Can't you see?" he demanded in a tone of supercilious condescension, "his cadaver's there on the plinth, in the back of the hearse."

As can sometimes be the case, this response was so extraordinary that, even when their every instinct and experience was telling them otherwise, the policemen were not disposed to immediately call Ron a liar. Instead, after glancing surreptitiously at one another, they politely asked Ron if he owned the roller and, upon receipt of Ron's lofty assurance that he did, they asked him if they could see the documents.

Ron then led the two policemen back to the passenger's side of the vehicle and duly produced his buff envelope, which he handed to the guardians of the law. One of them began going through the various papers whilst the other, after a brief stare at myself, John, Jimmy and Doug, asked us where we'd come from. "From the rugby club, officer," we almost chorused.

He rolled his eyes and shook his head sadly. "Why am I not surprised?" he asked. "But did you come here directly, or did you, perchance, stop first at Victoria Circus?"

We all considered this question carefully before shifting our eyes sideways to see if the others could offer any sort of clue as to how we should respond to this unfair leading question. After a second or two of semi-petrified silence, Jimmy bravely took it on himself to try and deal with this enquiry which might, if not handled with great circumspection, lead us into large piles of ordure. "Oh, we came straight here, officer," he stated firmly.

"From your clubhouse?" asked his questioner drily.

Another pause whilst we all racked our brains to try and work out where this obviously loaded question was going. "Yes," said Jimmy, not knowing what else to say.

"Along the London Road?" continued the police officer.

Jimmy blinked and tried hard to spot the trap which we all dimly suspected was being laid out for him. "Well, yes," he finally admitted.

"Then, since London Road leads directly to Victoria Circus, which is just up there behind you, how could you not have visited there first?"

We all sucked in our breath. The cunning bastard had caught us with a trick question. Jimmy attempted a re-grouping manoeuvre. "Well, yes, of course we came via Victoria Circus, but we simply drove around it."

At this brilliantly finessed response, we all nodded vigorously. The policeman looked to his colleague, now having finished scrutinising Ron's papers, and they exchanged a look of some meaning. Only trouble was, we hadn't a bloody clue what. "You haven't been picking flowers have you?" the first officer asked.

"Picking flowers? What us?" we replied in as injured tones as we could raise. "Why would we be picking flowers at this time of night?" enquired Ron. "Can you see any flowers, anywhere?"

After a hard look at Ron, they swung past him and walked along to look inside the hearse from either side to see if there were any flowers hidden inside. Fortunately, the only thing visible in the rear was Doug, eyes closed and arms crossed over his chest. Sadly, just as the police officers were displaying signs of what might have been confusion, Doug totally ruined the entire charade. Suddenly turning his head to one side, he vomited copiously onto the floor of the hearse.

Ron, having followed the police along the length of the hearse, then wholly lost the plot and aggravated the situation; he became incandescent with rage. "You absolute fucking arsehole!" he screamed at Doug, "Look what you've done to my roller!"

The two police officers were more than taken aback at this turn of events, particularly when Ron immediately attempted to clamber into the rear of the hearse with the obvious intention of causing the gravest possible injury to Doug. Suddenly mindful of their duties to keep the peace, they leapt after Ron to restrain him and prevent the execution of his loudly bellowed intentions of inflicting significant and lasting damage to Doug.

Thankfully, this last diversion proved to be a blessing in disguise as the police officers totally overlooked following up their earlier enquiries concerning the deforestation of the flower beds at Victoria Circus. Instead, we were all escorted to Southend Police Station whilst one of the officers drove the hearse to the carpark there. Then, after the duty sergeant made a number of almost original remarks about our intellectual shortcomings, we were all driven back to our clubhouse.

As to the hearse, Doug apparently spent a number of hours cleaning and disinfecting its rear until Ron had grudgingly accepted it was back to its former pristine state and then Ron managed to offload it to a small firm of local undertakers. Hopefully, it received there the level of reverence and care that were so shamelessly denied it during its brief period in less considerate hands; but then, Ron was a schoolmaster, after all, so it could hardly have been wholly unexpected.

AT HER MAJESTY'S PLEASURE

Generally, junior rugby attracts very few spectators, never has. Back in the 1960s, way before professional rugby union came about, the only games that attracted sizeable followings were internationals and other matches played at national stadiums. Sure, some of the bigger amateur clubs could probably anticipate up to about two thousand supporters to a game but, for most junior club games, one man and his dog would constitute a crowd. Indeed, for the lower teams of such clubs, they would consider themselves lucky if they could gather together the fifteen players to constitute a full team; anyone fool enough to turn up to watch them would probably get roped in to play. Maybe that's one reason why it was very seldom there was anyone on the touchline at such games other than grumpy old former players full of caustic, cutting and insulting remarks.

Strangely enough, apart from at representative games, the only times we could genuinely anticipate a decent crowd watching us was when we were in prison. Not for criminal offences, mind (not then, anyway), but in response to an appeal from some senior, social-minded officer at Springfield Prison, on the outskirts of Chelmsford. In my time, I can remember playing four or five times there. We only played them once a year as the Governor was disappointingly adamant in not allowing away fixtures. The games were always played on a Sunday and the selection of our team was never even considered until about 11.00 am that morning, when whomever had agreed to raise a team began frantically phoning around to find out who was available. Even so, when the rugby club opened at about noon, a full team was by no means assured and members drifting in, armed with copies of The

Times, looking for an up-market version of the shed at the bottom of the garden in which to gently genuflect on its contents without unnecessary disturbance, would find themselves seized by a modern form of the Press Gang. No matter their protestations, they would be grabbed by a number of those who had already agreed to turn out that afternoon, however reluctantly, in a kind of perverse pleasure in ruining someone else's afternoon as well. Sometimes, the intended victim would escape, mainly when he was accompanied by his girlfriend, fiancée or wife and had foolishly already promised to go somewhere or do something with them that afternoon. Not always, mind, as some wives often seemed extremely relaxed and almost contented about their husband disappearing for six to eight hours. Strange, that; until I became married myself, I often wondered why.

However, we usually got our man, especially if he was unthinking enough to confess he'd still got his kit from yesterday, either in his old kitbag in the boot of his car or, far more likely, where he'd left it, wet and muddy, in the club's cloakroom when he'd departed for the walk home at closing time the previous night.

Chelmsford was less than thirty minutes' drive away so, when the barman rang for last orders, our captain for the day would gather together however many players he'd managed to coerce into appearing and, having downed our last beers, we'd straggle out to the car park where we'd receive what seemed to be his largely incoherent instructions as to who was travelling with whom. Once this confusion was settled, between 13 and 15 of us would be packed into no more than four cars and usually less, and we'd set off for Chelmsford.

Now, some of those who were now on their way to Chelmsford had no idea against whom we'd be playing, let alone that we'd be doing so inside Springfield Prison. They just thought they'd agreed to a gentle Sunday afternoon run around followed by a convivial evening at what our American cousins would call a quaint old English Inn. So it would come as quite a shock to them when, in answer to their mild query, they were told we were going to a prison. Not only that, but this was no ordinary prison; it was Springfield, then a maximum security gaol, for Category A prisoners.

For those not immediately versed with prisons in England and Wales, Category A prisoners are "Those whose escape would be highly dangerous to the public or national security. Offences that may result in consideration for Category A or Restricted Status include Murder, Attempted murder, Manslaughter, Wounding with intent, Rape, Indecent assault, Robbery or conspiracy to rob (with firearms), Firearms offences, Importing or supplying Class A controlled drugs, Possessing or supplying explosives, Offences connected with terrorism and Offences under the Official Secrets Act." Not your common or garden criminals then but the crème de la crème, in other words. Not that all the prisoners there were Category A status; some were Category B. These are "Those who do not require maximum security, but for whom escape still needs to be very difficult". Whatever that means and in respect of whichever crimes that covers.

Since the journey to Springfield Prison was fairly short, the rest of the trip often passed in thoughtful silence, and any misgivings about having agreed to take part in whatever madness would occur that afternoon would be unlikely to be eased at the first view of Springfield Prison. Essentially, the first sight came when we pulled into the visitors' carpark and there, right in front of us, rearing skywards and all but shutting out the light, was an enormous, grey, forbidding, stone wall. It was exactly like, well, what you'd imagine a high security prison wall would be.

Whilst not as old as some of our prisons, Springfield carries that chillingly bleak, austere air that was somehow built into prisons constructed during Victoria's reign. They didn't want anyone getting the impression that it was going to be like a holiday camp for the inmates, after all. And if you wanted to film a remake of one of Dickens' darker masterpieces, then Springfield would provide the perfect setting. Although construction started back in 1822 and was initially completed in 1828, further works continued to be made at least until 1848, when a report about its use stated that "Each prisoner had their own cell where they remained most of the time with exception of visits to the chapel, or for exercise. They were not permitted to see or to talk to another prisoner; and no visits or letters were permitted in the first six months of their sentence. Mundane work was to be undertaken."

Obviously, a more enlightened approach to the re-education of offenders was being introduced. Even so, for the average number of about 200 prisoners it then held, the "Mundane work" performed was rather closer to hard labour, at least at Springfield, with nearly half of its prisoners having to spend at least five hours a day on such joyful exercises as the tread-wheel. Rather curious, really, when you consider how many people these days pay monthly gym membership fees to be allowed to voluntarily thrash their bodies on running machines.

Additionally, the distinctly foreboding feeling attached to the entry of Springfield Prison is that, from its earliest days, right up until the death sentence was abolished in 1960,; executions by hanging occurred there pretty regularly with, in some years, a good number taking place. This, then, was the fun palace in which we were to enjoy a Sunday afternoon frolic.

Having parked our cars, we'd be met by a uniformed prison officer, duly armed with an enormous bunch of keys. Led by him, we'd be taken through any number of doors and along various passages until we were escorted into an old, but reasonably light and airy gymnasium, with attached changing rooms, washing facilities and toilets. So far, so good, but all this occurred with almost none of the ribaldry that would normally pervade such a gathering before a match. However, that was all about to change.

Back in the 1960s, even before the RFU was run by what Will Carling would later most charitably describe with exquisite politeness as "57 old farts", all rugby clubs in England were strictly forbidden to play matches on Sundays. This was because of the proven danger (at least to the Secretary of the RFU and his eccentric, presumably ecclesiastical buddies) of putting their players' immortal souls at risk. No, truly. In consequence, the players (clearly all spawn of the devil) took matters into their own hands and, since playing in the name and under the colours of their normal clubs would bring down enormous piles of ordure upon any of what the RFU would view as being offending clubs to this dictate, we formed entirely spurious, Sunday only clubs. These nearly all had entirely facetious names, so as not to be too readily connected by the lame brains within the RFU with the clubs for whom the players normally turned out on Saturdays. As I remember it, Wasps were the "Commercial Road Travellers" and Rosslyn Park the "Red Hot Pokers", for example. Locally, we had the "Newts", the brainchild of players from Southend but which also included members from my own club, plus the "Winkles", constituting players from my own club, aided and abetted by guest artistes from Southend.

Not only did we therefore play for these shadow clubs with different names, we also designed and bought our own set of entirely separate shirts, often of garish colours emblazoned with suitably nonsensical logos. So popular did these independent entities become that their existence was further promulgated by the creation of their own similarly distasteful ties, the failure of which to wear one at a match would result in appropriately draconian and evening-ruining retribution.

On one of these particular matches at Springfield Prison, however, it all went a little awry. Well, a lot awry actually. Responsibility for bringing the Sunday team's own shirts was that of that day's captain and he, Fred, having only been appointed to that position for the first time, had somehow failed to grasp that this task was one of the most important associated with the granting of captaincy. That and the buying of the first couple of jugs, afterwards. In consequence, when we started changing and he was first asked, in all innocence, where the shirts were, he froze, right at the point of having removed one leg from his underpants and, looking fixedly at his questioner, said, semi-psychically already suspecting the answer, "What shirts?"

"The Winkles shirts, you stupid sod; what d'you think I mean?"

"Haven't you got them?"

"Why would I have them? You're the bloody captain."

By this time, this exchange had come to all our ears and the normal pre-match banter faded away as we also halted doing whatever we'd been engaged in, rather like a film coming to a stop. "You've forgotten the shirts? Then what the fuck are we going to wear?"

Another moment's silence whilst the gravity of the situation sunk in. "Well," said our captain, with unconvincing levity, "that's not a problem, we can wear the club shirts we wore yesterday."

To any outsider, on the face of it, this would have appeared to be a perfectly sensible analysis and proposed resolution of the difficulty. But that overlooked a number of fairly pertinent obstacles. Firstly, but of no real impediment (at least as far as most of us were concerned), was the possibility that, if we played in our normal club shirts, somehow those arseholes at the RFU would find out and visit opprobrium of the severest kind upon our own club officials. Secondly, and the real nub of the problem, was that it was highly doubtful that any of us had washed our shirts after yesterday's matches, which had mostly been played in dismal, rainy conditions upon pitches already glutinous with a malodourous mixture of mud and seagull shit. We all continued to stand there, motionless, whilst the realisation that we'd have to climb into wet, muddy and smelly kit, percolated through our group consciousness. "Oh, fuck!" was the generally voiced reaction, and we all began unzipping bags or opening the large plastic bags originally obtained from local supermarkets in which we'd variously brought our kit.

Sure enough, our kit proved to be as wholly repugnant as we had nearly all feared. The only person not faced with quite that situation was Alan, our flyhalf. In some ways, his position was worse. Being one of the big girls' blouses out in the three-quarters, although he'd carefully avoided being either a tackler or tackled the previous day and his club shirt had thus finished the game almost as pristine as when he'd taken to the field, he'd dumped it on his wife the previous night for washing and, wait for it, ironing before the following Saturday. As a result, since he was expecting to be handed a nice clean Winkles shirt, he'd not bothered to provide his own. This, clearly, was a problem of significant magnitude. Having explained it to our captain, he then forlornly asked this worthy what was he supposed to do?

Our captain stared at Alan with impatience only marginally concealed by his guilt at having failed to bring the proper shirts. "Well, see if anyone else has got a spare shirt with them," he responded and, turning to the rest of us, asked "Anyone got a spare shirt?"

We stared back at the two of them. A spare shirt? Were they insane? At over £20 a pop (and we all had to buy our own, remember), nobody possessed a spare shirt. At that price, we all stretched out the lives of our shirts as far as possible, sometimes for as much as almost three seasons, but by then their colours had faded and they'd been ripped in various places. Sometimes, if the rip was serious, say nearly a foot long, some half-hearted stitching had been attempted, mostly with twine, but smaller tears were normally left untouched, almost like battle honours. What's more, the sight of the pink flesh visible through these holes, seemingly indicating that individual's complete disregard for personal comfort (or even hygiene), was not heart-warming to any players from the opposition.

Receiving not even apologetic shakes of the head from any of us, our dearly beloved captain turned to Alan and observed, "Well, you'll have to play in your ordinary shirt; either that or without one."

"In my skin?" Alan responded, horrified. "Are you out of your mind? I'll get scratched to buggery. Either that or I'll freeze to death. And I certainly can't wear this shirt – it was a birthday present from my wife! And I'm not even supposed to be here this afternoon!"

Our leader shrugged his shoulders. "Up to you, Alan," and that individual, faced with such an invidious choice, slumped onto the seat behind him, clad only in his underpants.

The lack of sympathy for Alan in his plight was almost tangible in the changing room, especially amongst the forwards, within most of whom was a barely suppressed glee. One of our prop forwards summarised the best way forward when he urged our captain, now standing naked beside Alan, "Stick your prick in his ear, Fred, and fuck some sense into him."

Eventually, having had it pointed out to him that he seldom allowed himself to get near enough to any opposition players to run the danger of being tackled, Alun decided, albeit with considerable and loudly expressed ill-will, that playing wearing his wife's present was probably the less of the evils he faced. Accordingly, all of us having eased on our muddy, wet, sweat-stained kit with not inconsiderable distaste and complaint, we stood there, initially shivering, to receive Fred's pep talk. "Right, lads," he commenced. "This should not be a life and death struggle. Those of you who've played here before will know that their team will only have a few people who've ever played rugby; most of them turn out simply because it's something different to do and they can forget they're in the slammer for 80 minutes or so. So, let's throw the ball about and enjoy yourselves – show them what rugby's all about."

We nodded at him, but not really convinced. Just at that moment, the prison officer who'd brought us to our changing room returned, together with two other officers who were to be our escort onto the pitch. We walked along two narrow, increasingly bleak corridors, our studs tramping in wholly unsynchronised fashion on the concrete floors until we came up against a sturdy, heavily locked door that looked as if it had been installed from a Norman keep. This was unlocked for us and the three prison officers urged us through before, rather to our thinly guised concern, locking it behind us. Ahead of us, disconcertingly, stretched a barred tunnel that bore a striking and disconcerting resemblance to the tunnels through which lions and tigers used to make their way, snarling and belligerent, to meet up with their tamer in the large cage in the middle of the circus ring. It immediately put you in mind of wild animals and Christians being goaded into the Colosseum – not a simile that comforted.

The tunnel stretched ahead of us for no more than thirty yards, although it seemed a good deal further and, as we shambled out onto the pitch in our ill-assorted and filthy kit, a great cheer went up from all the prisoners we viewed through the enclosing bars of the tunnel. I say cheer but it sounded, well, and ominously hungry.

The pitch was clearly used mostly as a soccer pitch. It was not only marked out for that purpose but the goal posts had been converted from soccer to rugby by the simple expedient of wiring two long, fairly rusty scaffolding poles to the uprights and removing the net. The pitch was enclosed, behind one set of posts by the prison itself, with its gloomy bulk perforated only on very few occasions by tiny barred windows, and by two long, high barbed-wire fences along both its sides. Behind these fences were grassy areas about five metres wide and, behind them, two even larger stone walls, about six metres high topped with barbed wire. Immediately behind these walls were two watch-towers, one on each side, about twelve metres high, and each with a full house of guards, in the box seats, as it were. The fourth side stretched away into the distance, with an impressive number of additional soccer pitches available for the exercise and enjoyment of the prison's tenants.

Around the pitch were spaced about two or three hundred inmates who'd come or been forced to watch the fun, all of whom looked better if more sombrely dressed than we were, it had to be said. On the pitch, already awaiting us, were Springfield's finest, elegantly clad in beautifully clean and even ironed shirts and shorts, etc. We eyed them over carefully. Two or three had the obvious look about them of men totally unprepared for what they were about to receive and extremely nervous of whether or not this might involve significant physical pain and damage. They had probably been picked to play on the wing; a not dissimilar selection process to that we had also adopted. By comparison, there were three or four others who looked pretty useful or at least potentially dangerous to health. They had one enormous individual, at least 6'8" tall, who bore an awful lot of intimidating scars across his face, plus two or three muscular players who were sprinting across the field, throwing the ball to one another in a fashion that showed they were no mugs at the game.

The referee, whom we subsequently had confirmed to us was a senior warder, then carried out the unusual pre-match ritual (at least for us) of calling all the players to the centre of the field. There, in short, sharp, clipped sentences, more like a boxing referee, he sternly emphasised, "Remember, no biting, gouging, head-butting or grabbing of or kicks in the ghoolies. Anyone transgressing more than once will be ejected from the pitch and placed in solitary for a suitable period. Understood?"

We all nodded with considerable conformity, especially us. Christ, did that threat also apply to us? Or was it solely addressed at the inmates? Or was it maybe even a carefully worded piece of psychological warfare designed to boost the home side and scare the shit out of us? In some ways even more disturbing was his admonition to remember not to perform all the proscribed acts of violence; if he didn't, would our opposition otherwise forget to do so? Was that their default setting in a game like this?

Rather nervously, we therefore lined up to receive the kick-off. Unfortunately, it did not travel the then required ten yards so we all moved to the centre of the pitch for the first scrum. Normally, when we'd pack down at the first scrum of a match, both the adrenalin and the testosterone would be running fast and furious and both front rows would be leaning back, trying to restrain the maniacal hooligans in the second row, whilst silently glaring at and trying to size up their opposite numbers. This time, it was eerily different; both sets of forwards came together cautiously, very much in an "After you, Claude – No, after you, Cecil" moment. I could only presume their attitude was because they had a large number of wholly inexperienced players, whilst we were chary of being thought overly and challengingly pugnacious by a group of real hard men. After all, they weren't in Springfield for pinching sweets.

The ensuing scrum was the most genteel in which I'd ever participated. Ironically, the most savage and violent games, by contrast, were always those against any fifteen individuals representing the Metropolitan Police, over at Imber Court. At Springfield, by comparison, for the fairly frequent scrums held during the game, we'd all amble up, gently lean against one another and patiently wait for the ball to be put in. No collapsing on the ground cursing vitriolically, no snarled urgings to the scrumhalf to "Put the fucking ball in!" All very and uncomfortably gentlemanly.

The line-outs, too, had little resemblance to the unarmed warfare that ordinarily would occur. There were no sneaky punches when the ref wasn't looking or couldn't see, no standing on the oppositions' feet, nor tugging accidently on their shirts or giving them quick, surreptitious flicks in the testicles. All rather disappointing and flavourless, really. One reason, presumably, was the fact that we won virtually every line-out when, considering the leviathan they had in their second row, both sides clearly expected the opposite. Unfortunately for the prisoners, although their colossus towered over everyone else, he was not exactly well co-ordinated. And, even though his greatest admirer could not have considered him athletic, he was significantly disadvantaged by the lack of skill and accuracy with which the ball was thrown into the line-out.

Nowadays, the game is re-started at a line-out by a hooker throwing in the ball. This releases (so the theory goes) at least at international and at the higher club levels, those team-mates playing on the wing, who are normally faster, lighter on their feet and quicker thinking, so as to increase the likelihood of more skilled rugby. Despite the fact that, to a purely objective observer, this tactical ploy should be obvious, it took the game about 100 years to come to this same conclusion. In consequence, back when this game against Springfield took place, it was still the wing three-quarters who threw the ball in. Generally, this was just to give them something to do, along with recovering the ball when it had been kicked into touch since, in the lower teams of the small rugby clubs, the wing was typically the position to which you posted your less regarded players. These would include the partially sighted (contact lenses were still a marvel yet to be commonly available), the physically inept, those manifestly fearful of physical contact and those with little if any eye-to-hand co-ordination.

To be fair, we also had team-mates amongst the forwards who were less than perfect, such as those who were demonstrably mentally unstable, who were generally selected to play as flank forwards. There, provided they were carefully instructed as to who were on their side and who were the opposition and were then pushed in the latter's direction, they could cause a helpful amount of chaos and fear. Sometimes amongst your own team, too.

In any event, it was the responsibility then of the wingers to throw the ball in at the line-out and, that day, those given responsibility for this act proved to be a worse than usual collection of incompetents. Firstly, the prevailing methodology for doing so at the time was for the winger to hold the ball between his legs with both hands and to lob it into the air down a line exactly between the two lines of forwards. Forget all this nonsense you see on TV these days where the ball is propelled in by the hooker at considerable speed and almost phenomenal accuracy to a jumper who actually expects the ball to come to him. With practice, any group of idiots can do that. No, our challenge was much more mentally and physically demanding. First of all you must remember that the laws then didn't allow us to physically assist or lift any jumper. Secondly, none of us had a clue as to where the ball would be thrown, no matter what instructions had been given to the winger. It often went a great deal higher up into the air than it did into the field of play; and as for being thrown straight, well, the ball probably had as much chance of landing near the fly-half as the forwards. So, the Springfield giant had little chance of exploiting his great height. Even when, on the odd occasion when the ball was thrown in reasonably close to him, he proved incapable of actually levitating himself; he'd swing his arms with impressive energy but would only manage to get up onto his tip-toes.

To a purist, the game's standard of play was neither inspiring nor enlightening, although the crowd happily and dispassionately cheered the errors and obvious blunders as much as any demonstrations of skill which, sadly, were lamentably few. The biggest cheer came early on when, having actually got the ball in his hands, the Springfield flyhalf, a man of impressive girth and no little speed, hurtled directly towards Alan, him of the Carnaby Street shirt. Alan stood stock still, but waved his arms vigorously, presumably to direct the oncoming charge elsewhere. This had no effect whatsoever and the Springfield fly-half, snarling belligerently, one arm held stiffly in front of him like a jousting lance, drove straight into Alan like a runaway truck. To everyone on the field's amazement and the watching spectators' delight, Alan was not knocked arse over bollock but, seemingly impaled on his opponent's fend was driven backwards at an impressive rate of knots until, arms still flailing, he was flung aside as dismissively as a rag doll. The crowd found this sight exceptionally rewarding and bellowed with vociferous approval; Alan, however, lay there, pole-axed. Nevertheless, his assailant did not escape divine retribution as he tripped over Alan's initially flailing legs and plummeted to the ground where, landing with concussive force on top of the ball still held tightly against his chest, he knocked all the wind from his body.

It was a salutary moment. Both teams and the referee rushed over to gather in their respective fallen warriors and a hush fell over the crowd, mostly in curiosity. The felled inmate seemed, to any dispassionate observer, close to death, uttering strange, guttural gasps and making his best impressions of a fish out of water. His team-mates, after quickly assessing how serious was his condition, were wholly lacking in compassion and soon turned away, urging him to stop fucking about.

On the face of it, Alan was the more grievously wounded. He lay there, twitching slightly, as we gently sat him up. After waiting a few long seconds for any sign of sentient life, Fred, our captain, asked him, "You all right, Alan?"

Alan turned and surveyed Fred, his colour gradually returning, together with his spleen. "No, I'm fucking not!" he replied bitterly.

"Why?" asked Fred, "What have you done?"

"It's not what I've done," continued Alan, "it's what the fat bastard over there has done!"

"Why?" again questioned Fred. "Have you broken anything?"

"No," Alan spat out in fury. "The cunt has ripped me shirt all the way down – look!" And so saying, Alan held up his arms and we could clearly see that, right alongside the central seam, the material of the shirt had been torn asunder from just under the collar for at least fifteen inches. "What the fuck am I going to tell my wife?"

Ah, right, we all thought. It was nothing serious – just a potential domestic squabble. Nothing to spoil the game, anyway. As a matter of fact, the incident did have certain repercussions; the prisoner concerned tottered off shortly after, wheezing badly, to the jeers and catcalls of his fellow inmates, whilst Alan borrowed an old tracksuit top being used as a flag by one of the prison-supplied touch judges, to the evident approval of the crowd. After that, nothing of any real note occurred during the game. Ultimately, we ran out fairly comfortable winners, benefiting considerably from the evident reluctance of any of the smaller prisoners to tackle anyone running directly at them with clearly malevolent intent. When the final whistle went we shook hands with and smiled at our opposite numbers and were led back through the barred tunnel and grim corridors to our changing room. Awaiting us there, additional to our original three escorts, was a more senior prison officer. "Many thanks, lads. We really appreciate you giving up your Sunday afternoon to give our boys a game." Then, turning to me, he asked, "You were playing tight-head prop, weren't you? Did you have any problems in the scrum from the prop opposite you?"

I stared blankly back. "Problems? What sort of problems?"

"You know – did he try any funny stuff? Biting or nutting you? Or poking his fingers in your eyes, for example?"

I gaped with surprise. "No. No, nothing like that – he didn't cause any problems at all. Why, were you expecting him to?"

The senior warder pursed his lips. "Well, you can never know with him," he said. "He's a real wild man and we seriously considered banning him from playing, he's caused so much harm."

Oh, great, I thought, now he tells me. "No, truly," I confirmed, "he didn't try anything like that on me."

"Good," said the senior warder. "You didn't recognise him, then?"

"No; should I have done?"

"Well, you know the Richardson Gang, from South London described in the papers as the "Torture Gang"?"

"Yes," I responded croakily.

The senior warder nodded. "Even among other gangsters the Richardson brothers have a reputation as being especially sadistic. They specialized in terrifying other South London gangs by pulling teeth using pliers, but without any anesthetics; cutting off toes using bolt cutters; and nailing victims they particularly disliked to the floor using 6-inch nails."

An eerie silence had fallen over all those present, although the other warders were nodding grimly in grisly confirmation.

"And I was playing against one of these brothers?"

"Oh, no," the senior warder stated dismissively, "they're never allowed out of solitary confinement. No, the guy you were playing against was one of their enforcers, one of the guys who wielded the pliers and bolt cutters. Not Mad Frankie Fraser, mind, but one of his more enthusiastic assistants." He shook his head in weary distaste at the fallibilities of his charges.

I made no comment whatsoever. Nor did anyone else. The senior warder, his moment's light relief over, pulled himself together to go out and re-confront his duties. "Once again, lads, many thanks. See you all again at next year's fixture, OK?"

Yeah, we all thought, can't wait and, as the senior warder left, we glanced soundlessly at one another and, palpably deflated, stripped off our now doubly filthy kit and headed straight for the showers.

By the time we'd washed and dressed, the prison catering staff had visited the gymnasium and, awaiting us there, set up on three large tables, were a large tea urn, jugs of milk and bowls of sugar, a collection of sandwiches boasting a variety of fillings, plus an array of standard, thick white china crockery and some tin teaspoons. Those of us who'd played before at Springfield Prison carefully ignored the tea although those without any such prior experience immediately began pouring themselves cups of steaming dark liquid from the tea urn. At first, none of the virgin visitors spotted that only they were drinking the tea. Then, Peter, a very courteous and caring lad (don't know how he came to be with us, really), asked Sid, our senior statesman, if he'd had a cup of tea yet and, if not, would he like Peter to fetch him a cup?

Sid turned to Peter, shuffled closer to him and said, "No, thanks, me boy. I'll pass on the tea, if you don't mind and," here, Sid turned to see if anyone else was listening in, "I'd recommend you to do the same, too."

Peter looked at Sid, curiously. "Why? What's wrong with it?"

Sid shuffled even closer to Peter before saying in an even lower tone, "Well, it's prison tea, me boy; you know?"

Peter scratched his head and looked at Sid even more puzzled. "Why? What's special about prison tea?"

Sid drew back a little from Peter so as to look him full in the face. "You mean you don't know, me boy?"

By now, Peter was becoming more than a little concerned. He stared back at Sid and asked, "Don't know what?"

At this, Sid shook his head forlornly, as did a few others who'd previously experienced this rite of passage. "Think about it, me boy. All these dangerous men locked up in here without their wives and girlfriends for long sentences, what d'you think they'd be inclined to do each night in bed, all on their own?"

His attention now fully focused on Sid, his antennae twitching visibly, Peter said, throatily, "So what do they do?"

This initially private conversation had become more public by the minute as not only the older hands listened in but also some of the younger lads. Sid looked up and, seeing he now had a much wider audience, looked around, shrugged his shoulders, gave a sad little smile and announced, "They put bromide in it."

Peter continued to stare at Sid, obviously uncomprehending of the information he'd received. After a few seconds he asked uncertainly, "What the hell is bromide?"

Before Sid could answer, another player who'd been happily swigging down the hot tea, suddenly stared at his cup and, in a voice more than tinged with concern, said, "Bromide? Shit! It kills your sex drive!"

Sid and those of us who'd been through this little pantomime before all nodded, more in suppressed glee than in any real sorrow, it has to be admitted. "What?" demanded Peter once more.

"They add bromide to the tea and coffee in here to reduce your testosterone levels," explained Sid.

"Yeah," confirmed Fred, more directly, "to stop you wanking all night."

Although it was difficult to obtain confirmation or denial of this practice from the prison authorities at about the date the above occurred, it has certainly not been permitted since the early 1960s, since it has somehow been determined by geniuses unknown that to do so would be against the prisoners' rights. Try telling that to the poor sods working in the prison laundry. In any event, true or not, it certainly kept those of our community spirited team-mates who'd so enthusiastically gulped down cups of strong prison tea much more sedate and less boisterous than normal on the drive home. But then, maybe they were counting their teeth and their toes.

OH NO HE'S NOT

When I was in my late teens and my twenties, I was wholly wedded to my local rugby club. Firstly, of course, I had been completely and irrevocably smitten by the game itself from a very young age because of my mother's insistence that, if my father was to swan off to play rugby every Saturday afternoon in the winter, he would only be released out on parole if he took their eldest son with him.

Then, when I left school and officially joined my father's club, virtually my entire world, when not at work or at home, revolved around it. There was training on Tuesdays and Thursdays, Friday nights at the clubhouse anticipating the following day's game and subsequent activities and, on the Saturdays, freed from the need to focus on anything else as mundane and boring as work, I had the whole day, all 24 hours, when I could concentrate on what was undoubtedly the only really important thing in my (and presumably, surely, everybody else's) life. Sunday was for recovery, at least in the morning, before Sunday lunchtime refreshments at the rugby club and then another match somewhere out in the countryside. If this sounds a very narrow existence well, yes, of course it was, but to me and all my friends it was living life on the high side.

The point to remember here was that, compared to later generations, there was very little alternative entertainment. Yes, there was TV, but this was pretty drab and limited. It was still only in black and white and the largest screen I can recall being available then was just about 15". The sports coverage was minimal and we only had BBC and, from late 1955, ITV. These two stations expanded in number only very slowly and, even by 1967, when BBC 2 started showing just a few hours in colour each day, there were only three. As to the range and imagination of the output, if I tell you that the highlights of the week were probably Bruce Forsyth compering Saturday Night at the London Palladium and Liberace hosting his own show early on Sunday evening, you'll probably understand that few of us regarded staying in over the weekends as other than purgatory. Sorry, Brucie.

Probably the major single alternative for entertainment in the 1950s and 1960s was the cinema, commonly called the "Flics" or "Pictures". However, if you were an unrepentant aficionado of rugby union, as I undoubtedly was, this was only considered to be viable if your game was cancelled, and you couldn't find any other team or club for whom to play. Then, looking to gain some brownie points, you gallantly offered to take your girlfriend to the cinema. Unfortunately, it was only very occasionally that the films being shown locally included any that were equally attractive to both me and any of my girlfriends. Like most lads of my age, I was far more into war or adventure films, whilst my girlfriends would strongly favour musicals, a genre that, almost without exception, I loathed and dreaded. Some of my most cringe-worthy memories were of allowing myself to be persuaded to go and watch The Sound of Music. To be fair, it wasn't that much worse than many of the others but, having been dumped by the girlfriend who'd forced me to sit through it, the next female I took up also demanded that I take her to it. If I didn't, she declared imperiously, I could forget any hope I had of deepening our relationship. Seeing how, at the time, I had fond hopes and plans of expanding this into one of a far more carnal nature, I decided it was probably a reasonable price to pay. Wrong. Strangely, the young lady in question dumped me a very short time after we'd left the cinema, perhaps prejudiced by what might have been my less than thoughtful hints as to what was going to happen next. But, believe me, having to sit and watch The Sound of Music twice in rapid succession was excruciatingly naf in the extreme; no wonder I understand Christopher Plummer was not on speaking terms with his co-star by the time they'd finished shooting the film. Julie Andrews has a lot to answer for.

And, of course, there were none of the electronic gadgets that figure so prominently in just about everybody's lives these days, especially if you're under fifty. Or more than that. So most entertainment was generated by yourselves. And, as far as I and my friends were concerned, this centred around the rugby club.

So what did we do to entertain ourselves? Well, there were treasure hunts, when we'd provide what we hoped would be cunningly devised clues as to the identity of various landmarks (mostly pubs) which we'd then hand over to competitors travelling in up to about twenty old bangers loaded up with other club members and their friends, both male and female. These vehicles would then, dependant on their age and mechanical health, race or limp out of the pub car park which would double up as both the starting and finishing point of the afternoon's sport, and proceed to roar up, down and through all parts of the Essex countryside.

These and similar activities were arranged almost solely for our own amusement. Also, whilst they did indeed provide us with much personal enjoyment, there were those that also raised funds for the club, such as the monthly dances mentioned elsewhere. Additionally, there were others that were devised almost solely for the revenue they generated, principally amongst which was the annual Christmas raffle, for prizes mostly donated by, or squeezed out of tolerant members. Or, probably more accurately, out of the companies for whom they worked. Initially, this project, back in the 1950s, was extremely successful, but so many other entities in just about every sport imaginable climbed upon this bandwagon that, in the end, the only way I could find to sell my allocation of my club's tickets was to swap them with those being sold by other clubs. Whilst this meant I could justly claim to my club colleagues, with lofty pride that, using great effort, skill and cunning, I'd successfully sold my entire ticket allocation, I duly received my come-uppance when the club treasurer demanded I hand over the full monetary value of the tickets. Nice try, was his attitude, but no cigar.

But the social activity that I most enjoyed was the annual pantomimes we performed around Christmas each year. These not only raised funds for the club's coffers through programme sales and substantially increased takings behind the bar, but created a real feel-good factor for all the members and, to be more selfish, if I'm honest, enormous fun for all those directly involved.

I probably got the most fun and satisfaction of all, since I was the author, producer, director and bit-part player in these extravaganzas. Were they any good? Decidedly not; but then, to be fair, they were never designed to be. The entertainment that we served up was always intended to be amateur in the extreme, with the audience obtaining as much glee from the obvious considerable nervousness of the participants, their inappropriate casting and simply plain incompetence as of the total inadequacy of the plot and performance of the pantomime itself. The construct of these pantomimes was very much based upon the formulae used by the TV series, "'Allo, 'allo", suitably extenuated by the fact that, having neither professional actors nor even players who could remember even a single line of script, they each openly carried their copy of the script on stage with them and, when their turn came to speak, they would read directly from their scripts. Of course, generally having consumed a quantity of that elixir known as Dutch Courage before their performance, they were more than likely to lose their place on the script, mis-pronounce their lines, come in too early or too late. This was all seized on with great delight by the audience, who would barrack any such failings unmercifully. The audience, from the very start of each pantomime, was strongly encouraged to thus participate in each performance, aided by prompt boards to boo or cheer that would be held up by the individual appointed to be the stage manager.

All these events were first performed when I was still a player, back in the 1960s and early 1970s. All in all, I wrote six pantomimes, all based (albeit exceedingly loosely) on those whose names and contents are well known to just about every child (and adult) in the British Isles. These, like the originals, were inclusive of about eight songs in each, where I merely wrote fresh lyrics to songs that were popular at the time. I'm not sure, even now, that these new words fitted particularly well to the music and certainly their singers seemed to have insurmountable difficulties in synchronising the two, but what the hell, you can't have everything. Not that the audiences complained, mind you; they evidently considered such cock-ups just the job.

This all happened about fifty years ago and was only brought to a conclusion when I retired from playing rugby through injury in 1972, shortly before my wedding, And after that last event, I suddenly had to face up to my changed circumstances in life. I could no longer fart about in the same irresponsible fashion in which I had gloried for about a decade; I had new obligations to observe and this meant, inter alia, that it was time I knuckled down and belatedly passed my exams to qualify as a chartered accountant. It was time to move on to the next stage of my life.

And so I largely walked away from rugby for more than thirty years. Instead, I placed the vast majority of my energy and effort into building up my business career and, latterly, playing as much a part in the bringing up of my two sons as I could. Since my business career took me to living overseas for much of that time, and mostly to countries where Rugby Union is only a very minority sport, even if it exists at all, I only became re-associated with the game via the introduction of my sons to mini-rugby during a relatively short period when I was temporarily re-located to the UK. This was not through any deliberate action of my own since, being made only too aware of my wife's determination that the injuries I had suffered from playing rugby should not be visited on our sons, I kept very stumm about the possibility that they might enjoy mini-rugby. Indeed, it was only in response to a doleful, mute appeal from my elder son, Scott, then aged not quite six, that I assisted him in escaping from an activity that he seemingly considered akin to mental torture, namely Sunday School.

At the time, my wife was going through one of her increasingly confused exercises of the evaluation of religion; did God exist or not and, although she then considered that, on balance, he or she probably did, it was never very short odds. Furthermore, she couldn't make up her mind if, should he or she really exist, which of the multitude of faiths and sects had actually been awarded the franchise by him or her to represent him or her; and, therefore, which of the myriad others were thus actually charlatans. She therefore hopped, without any discernible rational thought, from one group to another, albeit without any real, long-term conviction.

Both our sons were thus christened twice. Firstly, soon after each was born, in our local parish church in West Sussex. I have no idea of what denomination this was and, from the very few instances that I, although a devout atheist, was forced by my wife to attend a service there, I'm not sure anybody else did, including its vicar. Some four or so years after the birth of Ben, our second son, my wife also had them both baptised again, in a very odd order that believed that such ceremony included each supplicant receiving a spiritual mentor who was a North American Indian. Don't ask me why; I didn't understand it then and nobody's been able to explain it to me since.

Scott had advanced to the age of rational thought by then and, after the ceremony, asked me to explain what had happened, and who was this Red Indian who would be guiding and protecting him hereafter through life. Sadly, I had even less idea than he did so we mutually agreed to take the fifth should we be asked any questions as to what had happened.

In any event, well before this last adventure transpired, Scott had been firmly entered for Sunday School. My wife, Susie, would duly ensure that, every Sunday, he was up at sparrow's fart, duly scrubbed, washed and dressed in suitably dolorous clothing, armed with a small bible lest he meet Beelzebub and/or his minions on the way and driven to the church. My job was to pick Scott up at the end of what he clearly regarded as a stultifyingly boring and useless waste of a Sunday morning. How did I know that was how he felt about this? Because he told me, with ever-increasing venom even as a small boy, every Sunday morning. In the end, I ended my attitude of compliant cowardice by broaching the subject with my wife, with Scott in attendance.

I waited until one of the times when her belief in the value of religion was clearly on a down-slope again and then, having mildly observed that Scott was not really enjoying attending Sunday School, asked her if it made any sense for him to continue. Susie wrinkled her nose and pursed her lips. She'd recently had a row with the vicar's wife and was obviously in a not unreceptive mood. "Perhaps not," she commented, "but what d'you think he should do instead?"

Scott's eyes lit up – was this a formal pardon? "Yes," mused Susie, "that church does leave much to be desired; perhaps we should send him to a different one."

Scott's face fell drastically, and I rode my white horse hopefully to his rescue. "Well, I'm not sure that Scott is currently old enough to appreciate and comprehend what seems to be the dogma that he's receiving," I said. "Why not let him do something else that he'll enjoy for the time being and then, perhaps in three or four years' time, we can re-visit the possibility of Sunday School?"

Susie gave fresh thought to this suggestion while Scott and I waited, both with carefully blanked faces. "OK," said Susie, "did you have anything else in mind?"

I pretended to give this matter careful, original thought. "Well," I gently suggested, "I understand that the local rugby club has a successful and very active mini rugby section – how about that?"

Susie's formidable focus, momentarily distracted by her contemplation of putting one over the vicar's wife, rapidly re-engaged. "I thought we'd agreed that, after all the injuries you suffered, rugby was far too dangerous for Scott to play?" she demanded.

"True, Susie, but hardly at this age. Scott and his friends are always involved in some form of rough and tumble, in any event. It's only when they get much bigger that the chance of serious harm increases; and it's surely better for him to be taught how to minimise any such injuries when he's younger? Anyway, why don't you ask Scott what he'd prefer to do?"

Susie eyed me with obvious distrust, then asked Scott in which activity he'd prefer to be involved each Sunday morning. "Mini rugby," he answered immediately, even though he'd no idea then as to exactly what that involved. As he confirmed to me years later, if he'd been offered the choice of Sunday School or shovelling shit, he'd have chosen the latter.

And so I started Scott on his own love for Rugby Union; and after him, my younger son, Ben. And, having enthusiastically accompanied them each Sunday morning to the local rugby club, I was not only drawn into becoming a coach to them and their friends, but also back into the general rugby fraternity, having retired from international banking and returned to the UK.

Not unsurprisingly, once I'd confessed to having been both an accountant and a banker, I soon found myself appointed as Treasurer of the club. Given that the despicable actions of the town council had, virtually overnight, deprived us of half of the changing facilities we needed, we had to engage in a desperate and urgent need to build a substantial extension to our clubhouse. This, of course, would require an extraordinary amount of funding, at least by our standards. Thanks to the enormously appreciated help, encouragement and generosity of East Hampshire District Council, the Rugby Football Union, the Sports Council and various other donors who wished to remain anonymous, we managed to raise almost £400,000 of the £500,000 that was ultimately needed. But that still left nearly £100,000 that the Petersfield RFC and its members had to raise by other means. So we fell back upon the time-honoured activities that I described earlier. And, as my personal contribution, I dug out of my attic the pantomime scripts I'd written long ago and far away.

Of course, they needed not inconsiderable re-writing; rather more than I'd over-optimistically reckoned on. I'd thought that all I'd have to do would be to change the in-jokes related to members of my first club so that, instead, they could be identified with various members of my new club. After all, the general plots (such as they were) hadn't changed, so how difficult could it be? Considerably, as it turned out and it was only then, forced to review their more minute details that I came to understand how life and society had evolved quite substantially in the intervening 40-odd years.

Nevertheless, having so loftily advised the General Committee that I already had 6 pantomimes that could fairly readily be re-written and staged to help raise the extra funds needed, I was rather hoist on my own petard.

And so, Sleeping Beauty was re-born .....

When I penned my original scripts, I was writing under wholly different constraints. My Old Boys clubhouse had commenced life as a bungalow in the inter-war years but some time before 1950, it was converted into a small, provincial dance school for little girls. When this suffered financial hardship, the rugby club, via numerous smallish loans from its some 200+ members, bought the property and, having installed a small bar, enthusiastically brought it back to life as a rugby club.

However, it was fairly small in size, with both a kitchen and toilets that were miniscule. Similarly, the space allocated to us in which to stage pantomimes was no more than about 8' by 18', inclusive of that occupied by the ancient, somewhat forlorn upright piano upon which our appointed pianists struggled manfully (or womanfully) to keep our vocalists as close to the chosen tunes as possible. In consequence, the casts of our pantomimes were limited (to Snowhite and the 4 Dwarves, for example) and we could only play to audiences of about 120, 50 seated and 70 standing behind, in front of the bar.

By comparison, my new club had been purpose-built, and less than thirty years ago. We therefore enjoyed the luxury of a stage that occupied about 12' of the entire end of the upstairs clubroom. Since we also had the extraordinary additional benefits of curtains hung from the ceiling, we could bring on players (I'd hesitate to call them actors) from either side of this stage, although such entrances tended to be from the side where they all changed into their peculiar and very personal costumes which, normally, functioned as the club's kitchen. Furthermore, we did actually have a stage, borrowed from alternative local institutions, which raised our players nearly a foot above the floor, so as to make them more visible and audible to the audiences of at least 200, both seated and standing. Whether or not such audiences thought this an improvement or not was never ascertained.

As I said before, the first of my pantomimes to be resuscitated was Sleeping Beauty. The amazing thing was that, despite the fact that we'd be playing not to a hostile crowd of total strangers but to people who were the friends, neighbours and relatives of the players, the players were all totally terrified. This also despite the fact that for at least 6 weeks prior to the big event, we had rehearsals every Tuesday and Friday night, after training. So, come the night, I had about 10 individuals (including 2 highly experienced police officers) who, when we assembled in the kitchen to don our costumes, were nearly all shaking like leaves with nervousness. And of course, to combat this deadly state, they had all already consumed liberally of the demon drink. Not only that, but Sleeping Beauty herself, a shy, delicate 19 stone front row forward with features that had seemingly been casually re-arranged on any number of occasions, had brought with him a large flagon of his father's home-made poteen. This was passed around the entire cast, together with the strong encouragement of Sleeping Beauty to "have a good swig". This duly occurred, albeit with considerable variations of enthusiasm.

Thinking ahead, it suddenly struck me that all this unrestricted and generous absorption of fluids could well have a less than welcome impact on the smooth performance of my masterpiece, a hope that was already severely lacking in credibility. Why? Because our stage was at one end of the rectangular area that constituted the first floor of the clubhouse whilst the stairs to the ground floor were at the other, and in between were our raucous, unforgiving audience. Why did this matter? Because the toilets were down on the ground floor, that's why. So, in case none of my stars found it possible to wait for half or full time of the evening's entertainments, and to avoid them urinating into the kitchen sinks, I obtained a large aluminium bucket from behind the bar and placed it behind the curtains in the corner opposite the kitchen entrance.

This ruse, whilst moderately successful, had a certain degree of mixed blessings. Have you ever tried pissing in an aluminium bucket in the half-dark whilst, behind you, a frantic fairy and a desperate heavy were urgently searching through their unaccustomed clothing for their male members before the internal pressures overwhelmed their willpowers? Believe me, it is a truly terrifying experience. Not only that, but the almost sexual groans of ecstasy that accompanied the near thunderous noise of jets of urine hitting the sides of the bucket quite silenced the audience seated nearby. Indeed, one small boy was clearly heard to tell his mother, "That sounds just like you and Daddy in the shower together."

Furthermore, my hope that by providing this emergency pissoir I could prevent my charges from perhaps urinating in places that would be wholly anti-social proved unrealistic. Having experienced mounting concern at the rapidity with which the bucket was filling up (and this before the interval), I was more than a little relieved, in every sense of the word, to find it empty at my next visit. But then a thought came to me – what had happened to this copious quantity of urine? Our villain of the piece smilingly confirmed his execution of his brilliant plan to resolve this problem. "Oh, I poured it out the kitchen window," he beamed.

Was this pantomime, this cultural extravaganza successful? Well, we, the performers, enjoyed every minute of it; and how. The audience also seemed to rate it as enjoyable and most of them stayed behind after the final curtain to buy us drinks and confirm how badly we'd performed and especially how excruciatingly awful our singing had been. Thus encouraged, we went on to perform 5 more pantomimes: Sinderella, Pouf in Boots, Snowhite & the 4 Dwarves, Aladdin and

Jack & the Beanstalk. As in all good pantomimes, the jokes were almost always the same, as were the innuendos and the insults, mostly about members in the audience who were sitting ducks and couldn't answer back. Accusations that certain individuals never bought their round were greeted with rapturous applause, clapping and stamping of feet, and not infrequently led to that person very ostentatiously standing a round for the entire cast afterwards.

I probably got more fun out of it than anyone, being as how I not only penned the scripts but also got to cast each of the characters. This was a self-feeding exercise. As I conceived which individual would fit each part, and received their agreement to the role, the character to be portrayed was melded more and more into the physical presence and behavioural patterns of the person concerned. This way, each character would find himself spouting lines almost certainly detrimental to his own image of himself, but which the rest of the cast would approve unanimously.

Even so, the favourite character I created came from no such source; he came straight from left field. In Sinderella, I opted not for the classical two domestic mice to assist the heroine, but for a rat and a visiting distant relative from Transylvania; a vampire bat suffering from asthma whom I named as Vlad the Inhaler. Armed with a pair of large plastic fangs and an inhaler (of which frequent use was made), Vlad was always trying to sink such fans into someone's neck, no matter who they might be, villain or heroine. This enthusiasm had to be loudly tempered by his local rat cousin shouting, "No, not yet!" whereupon Vlad's shoulders would drop in disappointment and he'd sulkily retreat to his cousin's side. This was a running gag with which we persisted throughout the show; once on the stage himself, Vlad would sidle up to any new entrant, cock his head at such newcomer and ask his cousin with ever-increasing hope, "Now?". To which, of course, the response was always, "No, not yet!" Luke, who played the part of Vlad, did so with the utmost conviction and even raised some suspicions as to his family's antecedents.

We had many other little jests of both casting and performance that I can recall with much affection. In Snowhite & the 4 Dwarves for example, 3 of the latter had to shuffle onto the stage on their knees, with carpet slippers strapped thereto. All 3 were well actually well above average height with Graeme normally reaching up to about 6'5", but the 4th Dwarf, being normally only about 5'7", played it for real.

It was events such as these that provided me with such joy and glee that has always rendered my association with and involvement in rugby so wonderfully enjoyable and heart-warming.

Long may it last.

NEXT GENERATION

When I retired from my involvement in international banking and finance in 2000 and returned to live in the UK, I almost immediately found myself drawn back into the world of Rugby Union. This was entirely due to the enthusiastic participation of both my sons in the sport. By this time, Scott, my elder son, had passed from school to Loughborough University and, whilst his playing experiences were mostly there at such time, he also turned out for Petersfield RFC when he returned at the end of each term.

Although this meant I had only fleeting opportunities to go and support Scott, Ben, my younger son, was still at school locally. There, like Scott, he consistently represented his age group at rugby and, in addition, joined Petersfield RFC's Junior Rugby section. Living just down the road from the playing fields of this club, I eagerly supported Ben and soon found myself participating in coaching his age group there. Thus was I ensnared back into the world of Rugby Union.

From then on, it was a very short time before I found myself becoming further and further involved in the activities of Petersfield RFC. Furthermore, when Scott returned from Loughborough University and enthusiastically threw himself in re-joining the club's activities, both on and off the field, I found myself almost re-living some of the happenings of my own youth, albeit now vicariously. In consequence, I got to learn of (and even participate in, even if only peripherally) a number of the escapades of, firstly, Scott and his motley collection of friends of mostly dubious intellect and then, subsequently, of Ben and his particular group of wacky companions.

When I first started getting myself involved in the general doings of Petersfield RFC, I suppose I had an innate suspicion that, over the lengthy period during which I had chosen to divorce myself from the game, attitudes and behaviour would have significantly evolved. However, whilst it was true that there was far more money available from any number of sources and playing and clubhouse facilities had improved almost out of sight, there proved to be very little alteration in the nature and attitudes of the individuals concerned. This proved to be most reassuring and welcoming for me as it enabled me to slot back into the fabric of the game relatively seamlessly, albeit I now fell into what was, to me, the once hated category of an "Alickadoo" or a "Blazer".

Nevertheless, a material difference that I noticed over the thirty year period was the number of players who were not local. With a town club, rather than an "Old Boys" club with which the vast majority of my playing days had been spent, this had always been the case, but the spread of their origin had usually been limited previously to the British Isles. With Petersfield (and in many of their opponents' teams), there was now a not immaterial percentage of individuals who had come to these shores from New Zealand, Australia and South Africa. Additionally, due to the number of British Army bases located nearby, we also had a number of Fijian players.

But it was the Australasians with whom I had most contact. Almost without exception, they all had farming backgrounds in their native lands and thus fitted well into the local employment pool. They were more than hard-working as they generally viewed the hours worked in the agricultural sector here in England as being pretty lax and far less than they'd experienced back home. However, the biggest difference in life-style, as they frequently remarked upon with some wonder, was the ready availability of a social life. Particularly in New Zealand, working out on farms some distance not just from cities but even small towns and villages, there was nothing whatsoever to do on weekday evenings; hence the acceptance of long working hours in anticipation of the weekly release of energy in rugby and socialising in population centres at weekends. By comparison, here in England, they had the opportunity to visit pubs every night if they wished to and, of even greater attraction, meet freely there with local females.

Most of these lads were charming, immensely polite and well-behaved; in some cases almost boringly so. On at least two occasions, Scott entreated me to have 3 or 4 of them join us for Christmas lunch but, although I was more than happy to do so, they were hardly the soul and spirit of the party. One year, we had Aussie Dave, Kiwi Tom and Tapa to join us, but they sat there, even the normally irrepressible little Maori, Tapa, as if they were at a Victorian Workhouse, and I was the Beadle.

One of them that did not fall into this category, however, was a New Zealander known by all as Gannet. What his real name was I don't think I ever knew; maybe it really was Gannet, but somehow I doubt it. Gannet was a wonderfully affable individual, one of those for whom the glass is always half full, although we all agreed he was a few bricks short of a load. Scott tells me his family had a large farm inland from Gisborne but had been unable to elicit from Gannet exactly what his role was there. Anyway, over here, he set himself up and offered his services to all and sundry as a "Grass Surgeon", meaning he cut lawns.

How much work came his way I never really knew as he always seemed to have been involved in some unlikely scrape or another, but I don't remember him ever being totally without funds. One of his most notorious escapades came whilst, for a very short time, he had installed himself as a guest with another of Scott's friends, David, a young farmer who raised a small number of beef livestock on an outlying smallholding. Entering the cattle shed late one morning, Gannet found David castrating some bull calves and watched with great interest. "Whatcha goin' to do with those testicles?" asked Gannet.

David looked at Gannet somewhat blank-faced. "Why, destroy them of course," he replied.

"Nah!" retorted Gannet, "You don't wanna do that. They're great to east – prairie oysters."

"Really?" asked David. "I've heard of some people doing that, both in Australia and the US but I've never really fancied 'em, myself."

"Oh, yeah," said Gannet, "My Mum either sautées or fricassées 'em for my Dad, but I prefer 'em deep-fried in batter or roasted. Here, if you don't want 'em, can I have 'em? Look, I'll tell you what, if you'd like to try 'em I'll fry 'em up in your kitchen, and we can have 'em for dinner tonight."

David looked at Gannet, more than a little undecided. Eventually, he nodded. "OK, but I've got a pretty heavy day ahead of me; once I've finished here I've got a number of tasks to do elsewhere, and I won't be back until about 8 o'clock tonight."

"Fair enough," said Gannet, "I'll plan on having 'em cooked and on the table at about 8.30."

And at that, Gannet grabbed the bucket containing the testicles and the two worthies went their separate ways.

As it happened, David did not leave the small-holding that morning as he found other tasks that needed his attention there, first. Having completed these, he returned to his house after about half an hour to get changed but was diverted to the kitchen by the smell of cooking. There, he found Gannet, sitting at the kitchen table, an empty but obviously used plate in front of him, but clearly in a certain amount of distress. Hearing David enter the kitchen, Gannet looked up and seemed to try and say something, but only emitted an unintelligible mumble through seemingly frozen lips whilst, at the same time, dribbling a copious amount of saliva down an already soiled shirt-front. "What the hell's the matter with you?" questioned an astonished David.

"I ips ar osen," answered Gannet, pointing to his lips.

"What?" demanded David.

"I ips are osen!" a now tensed Gannet repeated more forcefully, again gesturing at his lips. "Ook!" And, with that, he pulled his lower lip forward with finger and thumb before releasing it to snap back into its former position.

David stared at Gannet in both concern and fascination. "What's caused this to happen, whatever it is?" he wondered aloud. "Have you been stung there, by a bee or a wasp?"

"O, o!" stated Gannet emphatically, shaking his head.

David then looked at the plate in front of Gannet, still carrying smears of tomato ketchup and a soiled knife and fork. "Was it something you ate?" he asked. "What have you just eaten?"

Gannet looked a little crestfallen. "I ad oo ov ose alls," he confessed, a little shamefacedly. "I us onted oo ry ookin em," he explained.

David stared at Gannet, first in astonishment and then, as the reality of the situation burst upon him, with growing hilarity. "You fucking idiot," he said, "Didn't you realise that those balls will be full of lidocaine?"

Gannet regarded David with utter surprise. "Ot?"

"Lidocaine, you bloody fool, it's an analgesic we inject into the calves' balls so they won't feel any pain when we cut them off," explained David with a comprehensive and spreading grin.

"Ot?" repeated an increasingly horrified Gannet.

"Yeah," continued David, in between bouts of laughter, "and it takes about 90 minutes to wear off!"

"Oh uck," muttered a completely deflated Gannet, continuing to dribble saliva down his shirt.

Gannet featured prominently in a number of other escapades before returning to New Zealand, nearly all of them more extraordinary, distasteful and horrific than that above. However, because those who spread news of them by word of mouth had, by their own admission, been generally mentally incapacitated by excessive amounts of alcohol, much of such stories seemed not only lacking in credibility but were also totally improbable.

One last story about Gannet that I can vouch for though, directly involved myself. Having determined to return to his native land, Gannet decided to make an exploration of the US on the way back and, in particular, of California and the other Western States. Having learned that I had worked out there for a while, he asked me if I could recommend what places and sites to visit. So, one evening, Gannet came to my house and, having dug out a lot of old maps, pamphlets and brochures I brought back with me when I returned to the UK, I went through each of the extraordinarily numerous places of wonder that I suggested he should consider visiting.

One that had especially captivated him, even before he came to visit me, was Yosemite. And why not, indeed? So we spent some time on how best to get there, where he might want to stay, where to fit it into a greater itinerary, etc. So, as far as I was concerned, when Gannet left my house that night, armed with many of my old documents, he was as primed for his trip to the US as I could make him; he seemed to have taken in and comprehended everything I had told or given him.

Wrong.

About three months later I had virtually forgotten about Gannet. I knew he had finally parted from these shores so had virtually put him out of my mind. Then, at about 1.30 one morning, whilst blissfully asleep, I received a sudden phone call. Phone calls at such an hour are always a shock to the system. Firstly, you're violently jerked from the land of nod into an unknown reality, so your wits are neither totally about you nor at their immediate sharpest. Secondly, nobody normally phones you at that hour to wish you happy birthday or the like, so you almost immediately assume that someone is about to impart news of some catastrophe. So, still in the dark, I grabbed the phone besides my bed and muttered into it, only semi-coherently, "Yes?"

There was a faint crackle and a voice, only semi-audible, asking if it was me at this end. "What?" I ejaculated, "Who's that?"

This time, the answer came firm and clear. "It's me, Gannet."

"Gannet?" I asked incredulously, "Where the hell are you? Are you in trouble?"

"I'm out here in California; don't you remember?"

I stared into the dark, desperately trying to gather my wits. "What's the problem, Gannet? Why are you calling me?"

"Well, it's like this, mate. I'm lost and I've only got about half an hour to get to me hotel."

"What? Do you know what the fucking time is, Gannet?"

"Yeah, mate, it's 5.30 and they close reception over here at 6 o'clock, so it's pretty urgent."

"What? Have you rung me at 1.30 in the morning just because you're lost over there in California, five fucking thousand miles away?"

"Well, yeah, man, but it's pretty important, and you know this area."

I was truly dumbfounded. I lay there in bed, the telephone receiver pressed to my ear, wondering if this was some kind of weird, surreal dream. But no, Gannet's voice continued to bleat on about his bloody situation. "Look, mate, I've gotta get to Yosemite Valley an' I'm on 140, headin' east at the moment, but I was told about twenty minutes ago I should be on the Big Oak Flat Road instead. What should I do?"

I listened to what was all but gibberish to me with mounting incomprehension and then fury. "Gannet," I finally snarled, "listen carefully to me. I neither know nor fucking well care! You've got all my maps so sort it out for yourself!" And, with that, I slammed the receiver onto its cradle and lay there for a good fifteen or so minutes, cursing Gannet and his inane stupidity vehemently and sincerely hoping the bastard would be locked out of his hotel or whatever, and forced to spend the night in his car, as uncomfortably as possible.

Not unsurprisingly, Gannet and I did not speak to one another again for some while after that. Finally, about three years later, I received another call from him at about noon over the Christmas holidays. "Happy Christmas," he wished me genially, as if we'd never had a spat. "Look, mate, I've been thinkin' about that phone conversation we had when I was in Yosemite. About a month ago I told my Dad about it an' after I told him he called me a bloody bogan an' said I should apologise to you."

Bogan? What on earth was a bogan? Whatever it was, I was happy to be on cordial terms with Gannet again. "No worries, Gannet," and we proceeded to have a long chat about his trip back to New Zealand and his current role on the family farm.

And, having asked another New Zealander, I was advised that a bogan was someone thought of as uneducated or with only one oar in the water. Takes a father to know his son.

Relating stories like these is only a tiny fraction of the imbecilities that my sons and their friends got up to and, in the case of Ben, at the time of writing this, still gets up to. And, indeed, their escapades are far more exotic and unimaginable than my own ever were. Why do I think that? Because, firstly, there is far more money about than when I was their age; secondly, because so many items are far cheaper, comparatively, than they were in my time (such as air fares, for example); and, thirdly, the world is a much, much smaller place.

In my day, by comparison, a groom celebrated his forthcoming marriage with a stag night on the evening immediately before the wedding and it was generally understood by all those attending it that, additional to drinking as much alcohol as they could at the groom's expense, they would also contrive to get him as pissed as possible. Not only that but they would also perform all sorts of vandalism on his body such that, the next day, both at the wedding ceremony and subsequently he would be placed in situations of total embarrassment.

One such example was where, close to the end of the stag evening, when the groom was already only semi-conscious, he was stripped of his clothes and, in an act of pure patriotism, his penis was coloured white with enamel paint whilst one ball was painted red and the other blue.

Now, such colourful exhibitions of the inventiveness of the groom's friends still occur but the horrendous subsequent experiences of the groom seem to be a thing of the past. At the evening's end, in my day, at about midnight, the groom would be driven to his home, carried up the path in a wholly befuddled state and left leaning on the front door before his carers would ring the bell or knock on the door and scamper smartly away.

The groom, poor sod, was then left all alone to face the wrath of his parents when he fell flat on his face on the hall carpet when they opened the door. But that wasn't the end of it, not by a long chalk, especially as he had faithfully and with great solemnity promised both his mother and bride-to-be that he would not yield to the demon drink that night; not he, a man of high moral principles. So that abysmal failing brought about the first tongue-lashing, from his parents, albeit one that would fade into almost total insignificance later that day when his bride got him to herself. Next on the list of his calumnies would be the stern and often long-lasting disapproval of his new in-laws for arriving at the church in such a dishevelled and vacuous state, thereby almost ruining what was supposed to be the most wonderful day in their daughter's life, ad infinitum, ad nauseam.

Well, at least my sons' generation seem to have learned something about what not to do from such puerile behaviour. These days, not only do they virtually universally hold the stag night at least a week or more before the date of the wedding, but they do so miles away, pursuing the old advice of not shitting on your own doorstep. So, stag nights are held not only in distant locations in the UK but in places far, far afield, like in Dublin, in Riga or Budapest and not just for one night but, typically, for an entire weekend. My younger son, Ben, arranged for his to be held in Pamplona to coincide with that year's running of the bulls. However, whilst the stories that have filtered back to me have indicated that all those involved had an uproarious and sometimes hard-to-be-believed experience, remaining in the UK, I had to bear the brunt of his mother's incandescent fury. How had I allowed her beloved younger son to put himself in such a potentially life-threatening situation? Why had I not put my foot down and forbidden it? And not only that, but our elder son had not only even tried to dissuade him from this stupid, reckless action but had actually joined him - why hadn't I intervened to prevent this, too?

Fat chance. Although I pointed out that she had merely thought it amusing, nearly forty years earlier, when learning that one of my younger brothers had also run the bulls, and that, as regards this repeat performance by our offspring, our sons were (then) 28 and 33 respectively, this cut no ice whatsoever with my ex-wife who gave me a merciless bollocking over an extended period. Even after that, she refused to speak with me for some while. Oh, well, there's nearly always a silver lining.

So, although the considerably increased amount of money now available and the far wider horizons of my sons' generation have meant headline amendments, little of the underlying essence has changed. Indeed, the stories that my sons have related to me of their own rugby-related experiences, no doubt suitably sanitised so as not to shock my sheltered life-style, seem to bear many similarities to my own. Nevertheless, those are their stories, to be told in their own time and in their own way.

A SUMMARY EDUCATION

As I grew into my twenties, whilst neither my parents nor my employers would have described it thus, I became more responsible. True, I still failed to put anything into my studies other than the minimal of effort, and my social behaviour was, looking back, severely lacking, but what did that matter? In all the really important things in life I was progressing in leaps and bounds. Not only had I become a regular member of my Old Boys' 1st XV, but I'd been elected captain, and to that pinnacle of success could be added my selection for representative sides. Clearly, I had become a mover and shaker about town. Looking back on those times now, I cringe with embarrassment at my behaviour and delusion of self-importance. Trouble was, I wasn't the only one and, every Monday night, a group of similarly minded individuals would meet at our clubhouse to select the teams for the following week. What could be more indicative of our importance in life than that?

Our clubhouse was a building originally constructed in the 1920s as a bungalow but had been subsequently converted into a dance school by taking down the vast majority of the internal walls to create a large central space. Subsequently, it was purchased by the members of the Old Boys as its new clubhouse in the 1950s. There, each Monday evening during the rugby season the Selection Committee would meet to review the results of the previous Saturday and to select the five teams required to honour the fixtures arranged for the coming Saturday. Present were supposed to be the five team captains plus three non-playing selectors, all of whom were normally at least a generation older than most of the captains.

My memories of these meeting is now more than a little blurred; no one individual meeting can be recalled with any real conviction. Fifty years later such weekly events have run into one another but, for whatever reason, I can recall the bones of one that stand out more clearly than most that was maybe held in early December 1969 and, as usual, took place around 6 rectangular tables pushed together to create a bigger table about 6' x 12'. Behind them was the bar, being re-stocked by the Bar Manager. Through a centrally placed door alongside the bar was both a pay-as-you-go phone and a corridor to the toilets. I can remember it as if it was yesterday, even though it's probably actually a jumble of occurrences from long ago.

The Chairman, David, probably the only sensible selector, called the meeting to order, "Right, come on, gents, let's get this meeting under way."

Those not already seated around the table shuffled over, various glasses of beer in one hand and sundry papers in the other. All except Sid, our 5th team captain, who was engaged in a conversation behind the bar with Pete, the Bar Manager. "Come on, Sid," urged David, "You can talk with Pete later."

"Hang on, hang on," responded Sid, "I won't be a minute and, anyway, I've not got a drink yet."

This last comment was viewed as being of critical importance by everyone present and much nodding acceptance occurred, but Chris, the 2nd team captain was not assuaged. "Well, for Christ's sake get a move on; my in-laws are coming round for drinks this evening to confirm the arrangements for Christmas, and I've promised my wife I won't be late."

This unnatural desire to comply with his wife's wishes was greeted without sympathy and the others groaned and shook their heads sadly.

Dave, the 4th team captain, duly expressed the general reaction. "Christmas? What the hell's the matter with you? It's weeks away yet."

Chris, realising he was on shaky ground, mumbled something under his breath but made no direct response, and David again tried to call the meeting to order. "Come on, Sid, haven't you got that drink yet?

"All right, all right," called back Sid. "Keep your hair on, I'm just coming. Anyone else want another while I'm in the chair?"

Being perennially short of cash in those days, I quickly took up the offer. "That's good of you, Sid – I'll have a pint."

David leaned back in his chair in exasperation. "For God's sake, don't delay him any further!"

Sid ignored David and asked me if I wanted a pint of bitter and I happily nodded. Gordon, the 3rd team captain also piped up at that and shouted to Sid, "I'll have one too, Sid, if you don't mind."

However, a thought had crossed my mind and I shouted to Sid, "But I don't want any of that Red Barrel muck, Sid; give us an IPA."

"Yeah," said Gordon, "that'll be fine for me too, Sid."

Ken, our second selector, then stuck his oar in, much to the mounting annoyance of David. "I don't know why we stock that Red Barrel – it's piss poor. Tastes like it, too. Not only that but it makes me fart all night."

"Reet," came the dry intervention from Pop, our third selector, "Ah wondered who it were."

Pete then added to our knowledge by shouting, from the bar, "We stock it because we not only make more money on it but we have far less ullage."

David banged the table in front of him with his fist. "For goodness sake, are we holding a Selection Meeting, or not?"

Thus called to order, all of us slid quietly into our places trying to ensure not to irritate David any further and that worthy, having waited with a stern expression on his face until he had everyone's full attention, and proceeded to get the meeting under way. "Right; as usual, you're up first, Sid – how did you get on last Saturday?"

"Well, me boy," commenced Sid in his usual gentle tones, "unexpectedly, it was a close run thing and, in the end, we only managed to win thanks to a first ever try scored by Geoff."

Several heads turned towards Sid in some surprise. "Geoff really scored a try?" asked Chris in more than a little surprise.

Sid nodded. "Certainly did – I don't know who was the most amazed - him or the rest of us."

"How the hell did he manage that?" I chipped in. "He's totally dysfunctional; I've never even seen him catch a ball."

"He didn't need to, me boy," returned Sid. "It was a filthy day, played on their awful pitch up on the North Downs somewhere and we kicked ahead. Their fullback missed it completely – I'm not surprised, Martin was giving out on one of his Neanderthal charges, bellowing and roaring – and it rolled over the try line."

We all pondered this before someone enquired, with some disbelief, "and Geoff got their first?"

"No, no, of course not, me boy," said Sid, a little exasperated. "But it'd rolled into not just the biggest cow pat I've ever seen but into a whole patch of them – all fresh and semi-liquid, too. Rather like a chicken kurma banquet. And nobody else, either them or us, had got up the guts to dive on it."

"And Geoff did?" remarked Ken, in semi-astonishment.

Sid shook his head in a kind of sad amusement. "Certainly did. Came struggling up behind everyone else, pushed his way through and, before anyone could stop him, plunged straight onto the ball. Sent up quite a bow-wave."

At this, everyone else's face registered expressions ranging from humour to repugnancy and distaste.

Into the partial silence that transpired, David asked, "And that was the end of the game?"

"Soon after," Sid confirmed. "And just as well, as nobody would have packed down with Geoff. As it was, no-one would sit with him on the way back to the changing rooms. Only person who'd take him was Jerry, in the back of his Land Rover, and only then after Geoff had stripped off his shirt and shorts. Poor sod was nearly frozen by the time we got back."

"But you won?" asked David.

"8-6," affirmed Sid.

David then asked the standard question that was posed to Sid each week. "Anyone stand out as being worthy of going up to the "B" or higher?"

Not just the captains of the "B" and "Extra A" teams then turned to stare at Sid with a degree of suspicious interest. Sid had a knack, a history, even form for persuading players returning from injury to have a run-out in his team, often when their appearance in higher teams would have been more appropriate.

"No," Sid calmly announced, with a wholly bland face, "just the usual crowd."

This drew an immediate, sardonic remark from Gordon. "What, no-one at all, Sid? What about those three young school leavers? Didn't at least two of them play for the school 1ˢᵗ XV?'"

Sid, put on the spot, wriggled a little in his chair. "Not yet, me boy. They're still a little raw; haven't quite come to grips with senior rugby yet."

David, sensing the possibility of a little antagonism, quickly tried to soothe matters. "How much longer d'you think it'll take then, Sid?"

"Oh, a few weeks more yet, me boy," came the careful reply.

"Oh, yeah, Sid," said Gordon, with a little bitterness. "Like that lad you had playing for you back in early October? The one we found out had played for Wasps Vandals and scored a dozen or so tries for you? And who, once he'd been seen by Pop here, went straight into the 1ˢᵗ XV and has been playing there ever since?"

Sid gave a secret little smile. "True, me boy, but when he came to the "Extra B" he didn't know any of us and was terribly lacking in confidence; he needed to get out there and enjoy himself, which is what he managed to do with us."

Gordon shook his head, then commented with more overt bitterness, "Yeah, right. He could have done that just as easily in the "Extra A" and we were really searching around for a decent centre at the time."

David, sensing a fractious confrontation was beginning to develop, weighed in with what he hoped would prove to be calming soft words. "OK, Gordon, I'm sure Sid takes your point, let's move on, shall we?"

"Like he did the last time, David?" came the retort. "And the time before that? The "Extra B" are playing at home this week, why can't one of you selectors spend some time watching them and running the rule over these three lads? Maybe we'd get an unbiased opinion of their abilities then."

"Well," suggested Ken, "they'll be playing on the pitch next to the "Extra A" so why don't I stand on the touchlines between them?"

Chris looked skywards and muttered, deliberately just inaudibly, "Well, that'd be a wonderful solution – Ken has about as much idea of modern rugby as I have of Egyptology."

David quickly intervened to avoid the repeat of a long-held, bitter disagreement between Chris and Ken. "That sounds like a sensible solution, Ken. That OK for you, Gordon? And you, Sid?"

Gordon clearly thinking he'd at least had the point partly addressed, nodded noncommittally and projected a short stare at Sid, who ignored him and continued doodling on his papers, expressionlessly.

"All right," continued David, "let's move on. But before we progress to the "B", any news on availabilities for this week Sid? Or not?"

"All my regulars should be available, David," replied Sid, "and a couple more are coming back from injury, but no-one that should be of any real interest to the rest of you."

"OK," acknowledged David, "but we'll find more about that when we get around to selecting this week's teams. Now, how did you get on, Dave?"

Dave leaned back and smiled as he smugly announced, "I'm delighted to say we had a most encouraging victory, by 35-3."

Most of those present were already aware of this result but, even so, we all nodded with varying degrees of satisfaction. "Who did all the damage?" asked David with interest.

"Well," drawled Dave, "two young nephews of mine had come down for the weekend and, as it turned out that neither our scrumhalf nor our flyhalf could play, I was able to slot them in perfectly. Between them, they scored five tries and kicked seven conversions and two penalties."

As this report was given, all heads turned to gaze at Dave with increasing suspicion. "How many nephews and cousins do you have, Dave?" asked Chris. "By my count, that's at least six that have appeared for you this season already, and God alone knows how many came south to stay with you last year."

Dave shrugged. "Can I help it if we're all part of one big, happy family?"

"Aye," stated Pop, "we're like that, oop north."

I stared accusingly at Dave. "Talking with them afterwards," I carefully pointed out to him, "these lads said they ordinarily played for Birkenhead Park. One, or maybe both, said they'd played for Lancashire at some level, too."

"It's true," nodded Dave, "we're a very talented family."

"Are you sure, Dave?" questioned Chris sarcastically. "Only the younger one told me he was no relation to you, although he did confess you do all work for Shell."

Dave shook his head sadly.　　"You must have misheard him, Chris. Either that or he was pissed. Or, more likely, you were. Up north, we're used to much stronger ales than you drink down here."

"Aye," contributed Pop. "Thee's right there, Dave – weak as piss down 'ere."

"Well, I'm sure you'd know best, Pop," retorted Chris. "You've drunk enough of it."

Deciding this was getting a little out of hand, I tried to bring it all back to the matter in hand. "Never mind all that. What I find of more concern is the fact that when I met with Alan's brother on Friday evening, he told me that Alan would be on holiday for the next two Saturdays and that he'd given you plenty of notice. So why did you pick him last Monday?"

Dave looked at me evasively, with shaded eyes. "He did? I must have forgotten; and I only remembered something like that on Friday night when I picked up my two cousins from the station."

Gordon, now also suspicious of Dave's claims, said, "I thought you said they were nephews?"

"Uncles, nephews, cousins, schmousins," countered Dave with a careless shrug. "We're a very large, extended family. I can't be expected to remember exactly how they all fit in."

Pop, not to be left out, again climbed in with one of his typical irrelevances. "Aye, Dave, thee's right. I once 'ad a cousin, two times removed, who turned out to be a second cousin, three times removed. It were all very confusin'. An' another..."

David had plainly become exasperated at how the meeting was trending, so injected authoritively,

"I'm sure that's all very interesting, Pop, but I don't think it's relevant. Can we move on, please?"

Ken had to stick his twopenn'orth in, too, and muttered, sotto voce to Pop, "I know exactly what you mean, Pop. Back in the valleys, we all came from large families, too, and you were related to just about everybody else. Why, I remember..."

"Ken!" barked David, increasingly aggravated.

"Sorry, Mr. Chairman," apologised Ken, "but..."

"For fuck's sake, leave it!" snarled David.

An embarrassed silence momentarily fell upon the meeting before, suddenly, Chris rose to his feet, an empty glass in his hand. David immediately turned on him. "Where the hell are you going?"

Chris, in some surprise, gestured to his empty glass. "I'm just going to get a top up, that's all, David. Don't get your knickers in a twist."

David thrust himself back in his chair, shrugged his shoulders, sighed, and remarked, semi-resignedly, "All right, but don't be long; you're on after Gordon. But don't you want to hear how his game went? He might have some players to recommend to you."

Chris nodded. "Don't worry, David, I've already discussed it all with Gordon – I've pretty well already got my team picked for next week."

David shook his head sadly while Chris wandered over to the bar and ordered another pint of IPA from Pete, now placing new bottles of bottled beers in empty spaces on their shelves. David turned back somewhat wearily to Dave. "Anything else to say, Dave? Any non-availabilities?"

"Nothing of any note," came the answer. "I'll wait and see what players could be coming down and available for selection by me this week."

David then turned to Gordon. "OK, how about the "Extra A"?"

Gordon shrugged fatalistically. "We went down 17-0, I'm afraid. Which, given the problems we had with late cry-offs wasn't that bad. What made it worse, of course, was that we only arrived at the ground with eleven men. Sid helped out, of course – thanks, Sid – but we only took to the field with thirteen players."

David, looking puzzled, commented, "Four cry-offs? What was the cause of that?"

Gordon explained. "Well, Ian was confined to barracks by his missus; not surprisingly, really, when you remember the state he was in when we took him home the previous Saturday. What made it worse was it had been his wedding anniversary and he'd forgotten all about it. John told me she was so bloody livid about it she also gave him a good bollocking, too. Which he told her was grossly unfair given that if it hadn't been for him, Ian would still have been lying, face down, in the car park. Oh, and Ray simply hadn't recovered from last week's match. If you recall, that had been his first game for over two years and, on the Sunday morning, he'd totally seized up. Couldn't walk until Friday; had to stay at home all week. Lastly, we had two Christmas Shopping absentees."

At this last news, all of us shook our heads sorrowfully at confirmation of the return of this deadly, debilitating, wallet-emptying disease.

As a purely instantaneous reaction, I pondered aloud, "What's the matter with these guys? All they have to do is say no. Do it on Christmas Eve, or at worst, the day before."

Gordon shook his head in negation. "That's easy for you to say," he told me gloomily. "You're not married. You wait until you've gone the way of all flesh."

Being then a naïve (and unmarried) simpleton, I argued insensitively against what I considered his wholly wimpish assertions, in grumpy disbelief. "Crap! Absolute crap! You just have to put your foot down, that's all. It's not as if anyone actually likes Christmas shopping, anyway. Last time I was fool enough to get inveigled, I was virtually trapped into buying presents for people I didn't even know, had kids tramping all over my feet and some bastard with a Christmas tree shoved its top branch in my ear."

Gordon gave me a resigned smile. "Out of the mouths of babes and sucklings... You're lucky it wasn't up your arse."

"Oh, I don't know," remarked Dave sweetly, "he'd have made a lovely fairy."

At that point, from the bar, where Chris had finally finished talking with Pete and got him to pour him a pint of IPA, came the next disruption. "Anyone else want a top-up?" enquired Chris.

"Aye, lad," said Pop, "pint o' mild an' bitter, please."

Dave declined. "Not for me, thanks, Chris."

"I'll have a half of bitter, thanks, Chris," called Sid, "but not the Red Barrel."

With yet further irritation, David addressed Chris. "For Christ's sake, I thought you wanted to get home early."

"Yeah," nodded Chris, "but another five minutes won't make that much difference; sure you don't want anything, David?"

David wearily succumbed. "Oh, all right; get me a half of IPA, too, will you?"

Ken jumped in, as well. "And for me, too, please."

Shortly afterwards, Chris wandered back to the meeting, over-optimistically trying to save himself the extraordinary labour of making a second trip of about ten yards by carrying all five glasses at the same time, full to the brim. He carried the beers carefully, walking slowly and focussing his attention solely on the glasses but, in doing so, failed to see the briefcase I'd placed down on the floor by my chair and, having stubbed his foot on it, semi-lurched forward. Although he managed to retain most of his balance, he shipped a certain amount of the beer onto the six tables, thus liberally bespattering many of the nearer papers, particularly mine. Unfortunately, I was less than charitable. "Oh, for fuck's sake, Chris! Why can't you watch what the hell you're doing?"

"Sorry, mate, but I didn't notice your briefcase there," came the slightly abashed reply.

"Well, how big does it have to be for you to see it, you stupid bastard?"

Whilst everyone else pitched in to mop up the enlarged table and its wet contents, David tried to calm everything down and get the meeting back on track. "Come on," he tried to soothe me, "it wasn't as if Chris did it deliberately – it was just one of those unfortunate accidents. OK?" I nodded at him grudgingly. Peace having been just about restored, David continued. "Right; Gordon, given your result and the number of no-shows you had, I presume you're not recommending anyone for promotion, or are you?"

Gordon looked at him with surly disbelief. "Promotion? Are you kidding?"

David again shrugged his shoulders, this time in resigned acceptance. "OK. D'you have any likely absentees?"

"None, officially," responded Gordon gloomily, "but I've got at least three who muttered they might have to go Christmas shopping."

"Who?" came the truculent demand from all around the table.

"Phil, little Johnny and Fraser."

Chris shook his head in exasperation. "Fuck me!"

"Pass," calmly remarked Gordon.

"That's not mandatory, is it?" threw in Sid, in mock enquiry.

Chris pointedly ignored their comments "I can understand Fraser," he said, "as he's only recently joined us but Phil and little Johnny? Bloody hell, Johnny's a more devout atheist than I am. And as for Phil, I'll bet it's that new bird he's got!"

"Well," added Gordon, "you've got to admit she's a stunner, haven't you? Best looking bird Phil's ever pulled – usually, he wins the ugly bird of the month contest hands down."

"Oh," enquired Ken, "is she that tall blonde with legs up to her armpits and the big knockers?"

Gordon nodded with quiet enthusiasm. "Yeah – way out of his normal league. D'you remember that one Phil met down in the Old Town? Christ, she was ugly – what did you call her, Chris?

Chris smiled in reminiscence. "Pig with lipstick."

Gordon nodded. "That's it. And then little Johnny got up on a table to announce to the whole pub she'd been voted nomine contradicente the ugliest bird of not just the month but the whole year."

The entire scene suddenly came back to me. "Oh right; and didn't she go ballistic and crown Johnny with a pint glass?"

"Yeah," said Gordon. "Thankfully, it was empty, too – otherwise it might have killed him. And wasted a lot of good beer."

Chris stared thoughtfully at the ceiling. "And didn't little Johnny have to have about ten stitches in his head?"

David, with some impatience, brought us all back to the present, knocking on the table. "All right, all right. You can reminisce about it later; let's get on with the meeting. Chris, how did the "A" get on?"

Chris re-gathered himself and addressed the meeting. "Fortunately, we managed to squeak home 12-10. Slim kicked four penalties; two of them bloody monsters from inside our own half. We looked as if we might win fairly comfortably but then they scored two lucky tries in the last ten minutes."

Ken then interjected with some irritation. "I'm not sure that's a fair summary of the game, Chris. I watched this match and I've have said you were pretty lucky to win it. You only got out of your own half twice in the whole match and, if you hadn't had Slim to kick your penalties, it would have been a totally different result, see. You defended well, it's true, but the forwards aren't fit enough; a number of them were knackered long before the final whistle – that's why they scored those two late tries. I agree that Slim is an incredible kicker but, apart from that he's a bloody lazy sod."

Chris sniffed. "Maybe, but we won, and that's what'll go down in the records."

"Availabilities, Chris?" prompted David.

Chris considered the papers before him. "No notified problems, David, and we've been checking on the availability of the lads returning from university. I think one or two of those injured may be returning, too, so we may be able to cover the Christmas shopping bug."

David nodded. "OK. Let's turn to the 1st then. Pop, you watched this game; would you like to kick off with your appraisal?"

Pop, his moment come, looked carefully through his notes. "Aye, Mr Chairman. Well, we won, but that's about all I say for it. Passin' were poor; tacklin' were soft; and kickin' were over-done and badly directed."

At this less than complimentary summary, the others present turned, gently smiling, to glance at me and observe my reaction. I paused a moment, drew a deep breath and stared accusingly at Pop. "Well, where the fuck were you on Saturday afternoon, Pop? Because you clearly weren't watching the match I was playing in. Given it was on their lousy 1st XV pitch marked out on the side of a hill, where it'd been pissing down all week and also did so throughout the match, I don't consider that winning 25-8 represents a bad performance."

Pop sniffed at me, derisively. "Pitch weren't that bad, lad. You want to see a bad pitch, come oop to Yorkshire, or Durham; then thee'll see a muddy pitch. An' proper tacklin', too; not 'alf-'earted efforts. Schoolgirls could do better, in Yorkshire."

I turned to face the other Selection Committee members, deliberately ignoring Pop. "As I was saying, given the conditions, I thought we played pretty well. Ray, at flyhalf, had a particularly good game, as did Geoff at fullback. Also, it was nice to see how well Mike played, not just at the lineout but also around the field."

David chipped in with a query. "What about the flankers? You expressed some concern at their lack of bite, last week."

I wrinkled my nose. "No real improvement, I'm afraid. Chris, how are your flankers playing?"

Chris thought for a second. "Pretty well, actually – I can certainly recommend John; he's deserving of a chance to play at a higher level. I'm sure he won't let you down. But, although Brian's not playing badly, I can't let him go – if he goes up I won't have enough cars to transport us all up to Hendon. Remember, Brian can always be relied up to bring his Bedford van."

I nodded. "Fair enough. I'll take John then and you can have either of Tony or Brian. As regards the students, most of 'em won't be available until Saturday after next, I'm afraid, although there's an outside chance that Mick and John could be back late this Friday. If you'll sanction me paying Mick his petrol money, I think I could swing it for both of 'em to turn out for the 1st."

Chris looked at me in some surprise. "Why would you pay petrol money to Mick? I thought it was John that had the car, that beat-up old Mini?"

"Oh, he does," I explained, "but he lost the key and can't lock it."

Gordon looked puzzled at this. "Why doesn't he buy a new key?"

I snorted. "You know what John is like – he's so damn disorganised he can't get round to it. So he currently leaves it outside their flat with a piece of rope tied around the door handles and that of the boot. All you need is a decent pair of scissors and you're in."

Chris shook his head in disbelief. "Who the hell would want to; it's an absolute junk heap. And it doesn't help that he leaves his kit in there all week, unwashed. That's a pretty good deterrent."

"Whatever," I said. "Anyway, I'm therefore suggesting we pick the same team as last week except for Mick and John in the threes and John at flanker. If everyone agrees with that it'll mean that Joe, Pete and Brian will be available for the "A"."

David concurred. "OK by me. Anyone disagree?"

Everyone else shook their head and, having extracted a number of pre-printed postcards from my briefcase, I started writing out the name and addresses of each individual thus selected for the 1st XV on their fronts. Whilst I was doing this, Dave jumped to his feet and started to leave the tables.

David looked up, startled. "What's up Dave? Where are you off to?"

"I need a piss, David," Dave shouted back over his shoulder. "And I've got to make a couple of phone calls."

David tut-tutted, annoyed. "Couldn't you have done that earlier?"

"Come on, David," next shouted Dave from his journey to the bog. "You know better than that. A lot of the lads won't have got back from work yet."

"Oh, all right, we'll carry on without you. Chris?"

Chris spread his papers before him. "Right. Actually, it shouldn't be too bad this week. Not only have I now got those three coming down from the 1st but Alan is coming back from injury and Killer tells me he'll be available."

David looked between the two of us. "Alan and Killer are available? Shouldn't they have been considered for the 1st?"

Chris shook his head.   "No, they can both only play at home this week."

David turned enquiringly to me. I merely nodded affirmatively whilst continuing to write out my selection postcards. At that point, Dave's voice was heard, indistinctly, from the pay-as-you-go phone area.

Hearing this, Ken butted in. "Hold it, Mr. Chairman, I think Dave is trying to say something."

Chris shook his head impatiently. "What the fuck does he want?"

"What's the problem, Dave?" David shouted back.

The door to the corridor to the toilets was then half pulled open and Dave stuck his head around it, the old, black, Bakelite phone receiver jammed against his ear. "Quick! Anybody got any coins? It's ringing at the other end but I've not got enough change!"

The rest of us all grumbled but fished through our pockets to see if we had any spare coppers. "Come on! Come on!" bellowed Dave.

"Wait a minute," complained Gordon. "Well, I've got some but I'll need them for my own calls. Go to the bar and get Pete to change you some silver, you mean sod."

The rest of us, having heard Gordon's response, nodded in agreement and ceased ferreting amongst our change, causing Dave to swear and dash to the bar. Chris regathered his train of thought.

"Where was I? Oh yes, with those five now available, I can release Fats, Derek and Fraser to the "Extra A", although Fraser did say he might be going back to the Wirral this weekend for his mother's birthday."

Gordon stared at Chris. "Well, is he or isn't he?"

"He said he'll let me know by Wednesday."

"Oh, great," said Gordon. Then, after a moment's thought, he made his decision. "What I'll do is pick both him and Colin; someone is bound to cry off before Saturday so that way I might have cover."

"Right," announced Chris with some satisfaction, "that's me done."

Pop shot a glare at Chris. "What about Slim? D'you still want to select him?"

Chris glared back at Pop. "I told you, he's far too reliable as a kicker to drop him. Anyway, he'll never stop complaining if I drop him."

Pop gave something close to a disdainful sneer. "So what, lad? Are you frightened of dropping that great fat sod just because he'll give you an ear-bashin? Stand oop to 'im and be a man. Either that or get all of your lads to trainin'. How many of them turned oop to that last week, anyway?"

"How would he know, Pop," I interjected. "Chris seldom comes himself."

Before Chris could think up an answer, a fresh shout came from Dave, still on the phone. "Shit! I've pressed button A in error, before getting through. Quick, I need some more coppers, fast."

Pop carried on remorselessly with his interrogation as to the attendance of "A" team players at training. "'Ow many actually turned oop to training last week, then?"

"Four, I think. Mind you, we only had about twenty in total," I had to confess.

David was surprised. "Only twenty?"

For his part, and to no-one else's surprise, Ken expressed critical disdain. "Twenty? Back in Wales, we'd have got at least fifty and that's in a village of only 400 people, look you."

Everyone else, save Pop, rolled their eyes.

"Yeah, right, Ken," observed Gordon, "but all of them probably worked within only a mile or so of the ground. Most of our players work in London and it takes them at least an hour and a half altogether to get home from door to door each night. On top of that, the school is presently refurbishing the Gym, so we have to train under the street lamps on the grass section in between the dual carriageway. Strangely enough, though it might not have occurred to you, that can sometimes be a little dangerous with those bloody great trucks roaring past, especially in the pouring rain and when a ball is passed behind you onto the road."

"Well, as I said, that's it for me," concluded Chris.

Gordon shifted his attention back to his own selection responsibilities. "So, what have I got? Let's see." At this point, as Gordon started sorting through his papers, Dave came back from making his phone calls and, contemporaneously, both Chris and I got up from our seats. Additionally, the side door to the clubhouse swung open and in came the club's fixtures secretary, Barry.

David called out, in further exasperation, "Now what the hell's going on? Where are you to off to, Chris, for starters?"

"Like I told you, David, I've got to get home early tonight to meet with my in-laws – I've selected my team for Saturday and written out all my cards so there's no real point in my staying any longer."

I looked at Chris with some suspicion. "Yeah, right. I'll bet that's all a load of bollocks – I'll bet you're just on a bloody promise tonight."

Chris beamed at me with smug superiority, gave me a V sign and hurried out. I watched him go and then turned back to those still remaining. "It's my shout, guys – what are you having, David? Another half?"

Barry strode energetically over to join us. "Evenin' all, spot of bad news, I'm afraid – the "B" team fixture for Saturday is cancelled. Opposition can't raise a team, especially as it's over here and Christmas shopping duties are being laid down. Oh, and I'll have a pint of IPA please," he added, for my benefit.

Dave threw his pencil onto the table. "Oh, for fuck's sake. Those bastards do this every bloody year. I'll bet you they'll be able to raise a team next year, when we'll be playing over there. Barry, can you rustle up a fixture against another club?"

David raised his hand for me. "Yes, I'll have another half – thanks."

"Me, too," quickly added Ken.

Barry concentrated on the fixture situation of the "B". "I'll have a go on Thursday, Dave, at the Exchange. Any team to which you've got strong objections?"

Pop woke up suddenly to my offer. "Another pint o' mild and bitter for me, lad."

Dave gave some thought to Barry's question. "Not really, just as long as it's not bloody miles away, like that last-minute fixture you arranged for us in October, down in Sussex."

"Sorry, Dave, but as I said to you then, it was all I could get."

"Yeah, but you were conned, old son. You told me it was on the edge of Sussex but what you didn't tell us was it was on the southern edge, right by the fucking Channel."

Barry shrugged without concern; as a life-long "Ex B" stalwart it wouldn't be his problem. "Oh, well, you win some, you lose some." He turned back to me. "Oh, I've been asked if we'd like to host that team from Durham again this Easter – any interest?"

I wrinkled my brow. "That mob from some mining village, weren't they?"

Gordon grinned. "Rather you than me – they were an evil-looking bunch. All about 5'10", from scrumhalf to second row, and all looking as if someone had re-arranged their features with a shovel."

Pop nodded approvingly. "Aye, good lads, they were."

I sniffed. "I don't know about good, but they were bloody hard. Even so, at least they wanted to play rugby, unlike the Irish who've come across to play us at Easter or, worse still, the Welsh. The Irish just want an eighty minute punch-up but at least they're open and honest about it. Not like the fucking Welsh; they make sure both you and the referee aren't looking when they lay into you – bastards."

Ken smiled condescendingly. "Well now, you're only saying that because we beat you every time."

Dave shook his head dismissively. "Oh, piss off, Ken."

"Go on then, when did you last beat us? And how many times has England beaten Wales since 1960? That's in eight years mind. Can't remember? Well, I'll tell you – just twice; and they were both against the run of play. And you only won three times in the previous ten years, too."

I shrugged in tired acknowledgement at this bitter but unchallengeable truth. "Yeah, all right, Ken, but that doesn't mean that your club teams aren't bloody dirty."

David, sensing things might be getting a little out of hand butted in. "All right guys, enough's enough – let's get back to selection. Barry, why don't the two of you decide whether or not to accept this Durham fixture later? And where are we with the remainder of this week's selection? Gordon?"

Barry and I having left the meeting, our roles having been completed, Ken and Pop also moved off to drink at the bar since they've already been assigned which teams they'd watch on the coming Saturday afternoon. Whilst their meeting within a meeting got under way, Pete, who'd been rummaging around beneath the bar, suddenly give a loud snort of disbelief and straightened up, holding a woman's bra up aloft. "Hey!" he shouted. "Look at this! Anyone got any idea where this has come from?"

All heads swung round to see what Pete was referring to and Barry reached up to take it from Pete. Having examined the article carefully, and then sniffed inside the cups, Barry gave us all his formal expert opinion. "Well, she's a big girl, whomever she is. Uses Imperial Leather, too."

The remaining attendees at the table shook their heads and huddled together to sort out the remaining three teams even though there might not be a match for the "B" XV. This closely resembled a game of poker, with each of the two lower team captains trying as hard as possible not to reveal the identity of any returning or new player who could not only strengthen the performance of their own team but, in all probability, that of any team above. Another important consideration to throw into this mix was not only the availability of players with vehicles that could be used to transport players to the away matches, no matter how little ability they might have to play rugby, but also whether or not they could be encouraged not to return early, and whether or not they could be persuaded to grossly overload their vehicles, especially on the way home. This resulted in a good deal of horse trading which would not only affect the coming Saturday's selection, but could also be carried forward like an unpaid obligation into the future. Finally, all the requisite decisions were made, even if more than a little unwillingly at times, and everyone headed to the bar for a more convivial end to the evening.

These and similar experiences, as I'm sure you'll agree, I considered to be a very important aspect of my education in life. Look where it got me.

CPSIA information can be obtained
at www.ICGtesting.com
Printed in the USA
LVHW042343230719
625094LV00001B/17

9 781643 617336